ISIS

QUEEN OF EGYPTIAN MAGIC

HER BOOK OF DIVINATION AND SPELLS

JONATHAN DEE

CICO BOOKS

London

Contents

Picture List

Front cover: Inlay of a face in red jasper, possibly that of Isis (18th/19th dynasty, uncertain). Werner Forman Archive/ex-Schimmel Collection, New York.

Back cover: Seti I as Osiris. Relief in Temple of Seti, Hyopstyle Hall, Abydos. AKG London/Erich Lessing.

Back flap: Bronze figurine of Bast. Louvre Museum, Paris. AKG London/Erich Lessing.

1 Isis. Private collection.

2 A detail of a wall painting in the tomb of Amen-hor-khepeshef, the goddess Hathor/Isis faces Ramesses III (20th dynasty; c. 1190–1160 BCE). Werner Forman Archive/E. Strouhal.

6 The sky goddess Nut devours the sun, from the burial chamber of the tomb of Ramesses III (20th dynasty; c. 1126–1108 BCE). Werner Forman Archive/E. Strouhal.

10 The sky goddess Nut. Private collection.

11 A fragment of a Middle Kingdom relief showing Seth holding an ankh and presenting the seated pharaoh with a symbol representing eternity. Werner Forman Archive/The Egyptian Museum, Cairo.

12 Relief detail depicting the goddess Nut, from the lid of the sarcophagus of Sety I. (19th dynasty, c. 1294–1279 BCE). Werner Forman Archive/Sir John Soane's Museum, London.

14 A detail of a wall painting in the tomb of Amen-hor-khepeshef. Ptah, the god of creation, shrouded in mummy wrappings stands within a sarcophagus (20th dynasty; c. 1190–1160 BCE). Werner Forman Archive/E. Strouhal.

17 A relief in the tomb of Mereruka (6th dynasty; c. 2345–2323 BCE). Werner Forman Archive/The Egyptian Museum, Cairo.

19 Relief on a fallen obelisk at Karnak. Queen Hatshepsut, depicted as a Pharaoh, is crowned by Amun (18th dynasty). Werner Forman Archive.

21 Detail from the coffin of Nespawershepi, chief scribe of the temple of Amun (21st dynasty; c. 984 BCE). Werner Forman Archive/Fitzwilliam Museum, Cambridge.

23 Detail of a painting in the tomb of Sannedjem. A musician entertains the deceased and his wife. E. Strouhal.

24 A detail from the private tomb of the royal tomb builder, Pashedu (19th dynasty; c. 1295–1186 BCE). E. Strouhal.

25 The hand of King Akhenaten, dropping unguent on the offerings to Aten (18th dynasty; c.1352–1336 BCE). Werner Forman Archive/The Schimmel Collection, New York.

26 Detail of a relief from the temple of King Unas at Saqqara. Unas is suckled by an unknown goddess (5th dynasty; c. 2494–2345 BCE). Werner Forman Archive/The Egyptian Museum, Cairo.

28 A sketch of a crane, a vulture, and a basenji. Werner Forman Archive/The Egyptian Museum, Cairo.

29 Bust thought to be of King Amenemhat IV (12th dynasty; c. 1808–1799 BCE). Werner Forman Archive/Collection of George Ortiz, Vandoeuvres.

33 A vignette from *The Book of the Dead of Nakhte*: the important scribe and his wife stand before Osiris in the garden of their house (18th dynasty; c. 1550–1295 BCE). Werner Forman Archive/The British Museum, London.

34 Relief carving showing wheat (18th dynasty; c. 1352–1336 BCE). Werner Forman Archive/ The Schimmel Collection, New York.

36 An uninscribed head found near the sun temple of King Userkaf at Abusir and thought to represent the king (5th dynasty; c. 2500–2350 BCE). Werner Forman Archive/The Egyptian Museum, Cairo.

39 Gold plaque found with the mummified body of King Psusennes I: the eye of Horus is a symbol of restoration intact in the afterlife (21st dynasty; c. 1039–991 BCE). Werner Forman Archive/The Egyptian Museum, Cairo.

40 Sheet gold amulet of Osiris standing on the hieroglyph "m" for Maat, or universal truth and order (22nd dynasty; c. 874–850 BCE). Werner Forman Archive/The Egyptian Museum, Cairo.

42 Bronze figure of Sekhmet, a goddess of war, sorcery and healing (c. 600 BCE). Werner Forman Archive/Christie's, London.

43 Polished bronze mirror incorporating a double-sided image of the goddess Hathor (16th dynasty; c. 1550–1295 BCE). Werner Forman Archive/The Egyptian Museum, Cairo.

44 Gold relief mask of the goddess Hathor (c. 200–0 BCE). Werner Forman Archive/The Royal Athena Gallery, New York.

47 Alabaster statue, probably produced in a royal workshop (4th–5th dynasty). Werner Forman Archive/The British Museum, London.

49 Vignette from *The Book of the Dead of Neferrenpet*: the body and soul represented by the ba bird, are reunited (19th dynasty; c. 1295–1186 BCE). Werner Forman Archive/Musees Royaux du Cinquantenaire, Brussels.

50 Detail of a wall painting in the tomb of Horemheb. Hathor/Isis faces the pharaoh. Werner Forman Archive/E. Strouhal.

53 A detail of a wall painting in the tomb of Menna showing the harvesting of wheat, here the surveyors measure the crop before it is cut (18th dynasty; c. 1400–1350 BCE). Werner Forman Archive.

54 Detail of a fragment of a palette used for grinding eye-paint, it shows a lion, and vultures preying on bodies after battle. Werner Forman Archive/The

British Museum, London.

56 A fragment of a relief with the figures of two princesses (18th dynasty; c. 1352–1336 BCE). Werner Forman Archive/The Schimmel Collection, New York.

59 Cosmetic dish with a handle carved in the form of a swimming girl. The container is in the shape of a duck (19th dynasty). Werner Forman Archive/The British Museum, London.

61 Sculpture in Egyptian blue, a material closely allied to glass. Seated on a throne, Isis suckles the infant Horus (18th dynasty; c. 1400–1379 BCE). Werner Forman Archive/The Schimmel Collection, New York.

62 A detail from the coffin of Nespawershepi, chief scribe of the temple of Amun. The sky goddess Nut drops rain on Osiris bringing forth seedlings (21st dynasty; c. 984 BCE). Werner Forman Archive/ Fitzwilliam Museum, Cambridge.

63 A detail of the statues of Prince Rahotep and his wife Nofret. This close view of Nofret shows her jewelry, costume, and wig (4th dynasty; c. 2613–2494 BCE). Werner Forman Archive/The Egyptian Museum, Cairo.

64 Model of a rowing boat with crew and steering posts, carved to look like a skiff made of papyrus reeds (6th dynasty; c. 2345–2181 BCE). Werner Forman Archive/The British Museum, London.

65 Detail of a painting in the tomb of Sennedjem, who with his wife pays homage before a shrine to the gods of the underworld (19th dynasty; c. 1295–1186 BCE). Werner Forman Archive/E. Strouhal.

67 A detail of a painting in the tomb of Sennedjem. The deceased prays in front of a god of the underworld who adopts the form of a lion (19th dynasty; c. 1295–1186 BCE). E. Strouhal.

68 A statuette of a young woman wearing a wig and a broad collar (18–20th dynasty). Werner Forman Archive/private collection.

69 Head of silver coffin of Psusennes I from the royal necropolis at Tanis (21st dynasty; 1039–991 BCE). Werner Forman Archive/The Egyptian Museum, Cairo.

70 Gold funerary mask for the burial of Psusennes I (21st dynasty 1039–991 BCE). Werner Forman Archive/The Egyptian Museum, Cairo.

72 A relief from King Djet's tomb at Abydos. Horus sits above a snake on a monument carved in relief (21st dynasty; c. 3100–2890 BCE). Werner Forman Archive/Musee du Louvre, Paris.

74 Detail from a coffin depicting Osiris, the god of the dead (21st or 22nd dynasty). Werner Forman Archive/The British Museum, London.

75 A slab-stela depicting Princess Nefertiabt dressed as a priestess in a panther skin, seated before an offering table (4th dynasty; c. 2613–2494 bc) Werner

Forman Archive/Louvre Museum, Paris.

76 Roman period gilt coffin. Detail of foot showing Isis and Nephthys lamenting over the murdered Osiris (c. 100 BCE). Werner Forman Archive/Museum of Fine Arts, Boston.

78 A detail from the wall painting in the tomb of queen Nefertari. Hathor/Isis leads the queen by the hand (19th dynasty; c. 1290–1220 BCE). Werner Forman Archive/E. Strouhal.

81 One of six panels from the altar of Hesire, a high official of King Zoser who was Chief of Dentists, and Physicians (3rd dynasty; c. 2700–2600 BCE). Werner Forman Archive/The Egyptian Museum, Cairo.

85 Miniature blue glass paste head of the pharaoh Amenophis III, wearing the blue, or war, crown (18th dynasty; c. 1390–1352 BCE). Werner Forman Archive/Calouste Gulbenkian Museum, Lisbon.

85 An alabaster panel decorated with a profile head and torso of Rawer. It was found in his tomb at Giza (5th dynasty; 2494–2345 BCE). Werner Forman Archive/The Egyptian Museum, Cairo.

87 Horus falcon. Werner Forman Archive/Schimmel Collection, New York.

88 "Wedjat eye" pendant from the tomb of Tuthankhamun (18th dynasty; c. 1336–1327 BCE). Werner Forman Archive/The Egyptian Museum, Cairo.

90 Reliefs such as this example, depicting Horus standing on two crocodiles, were intended to prevent attacks by harmful creatures as well as cure snakebites, and scorpion stings. Werner Forman Archive/Ariadne Gallery, New York.

91 Cosmetic spoon in the form of young women in a papyrus thicket supporting a vessel heaped with unguent (18th dynasty; c. 1375 BCE). Werner Forman Archive/Ny Carlberg Glyptotek, Copenhagen.

94 Painted relief from the tomb of Nefertari representing the sky-bull and three of the seven sacred "Hathor cows" (19th dynasty, c. 1290–1220 BCE). Werner Forman Archive/E. Strouhal.

95 Part of the Narmer palette which commemorates the victories of King Narmer or King Memes, the unifier of Upper and Lower Egypt (1st dynasty; c. 3100–2890 BCE). Werner Forman Archive/The Egyptian Museum, Cairo.

96 Fragment of the "Battlefield Palette"; decorated with a guinea-fowl and perhaps a gazelle. Werner Forman Archive/Ashmoleon Museum, Oxford.

97 A detail from the lid of a casket of Tuthankhamun showing the king (18th dynasty; c. 1357–1349 BCE). Werner Forman Archive/The Egyptian Museum, Cairo.

99 Detail from the Book of the Dead of Nebqed: arrival of the deceased in the court of the deity of the afterlife (18th dynasty; c. 1400 BCE). Werner Forman Archive/Louvre Museum, Paris.

100 The uraeas, the royal cobra of Ancient Egypt, was worn by the pharaoh on his brow, usually with a royal crown, as a symbol of his

supreme authority. Werner Forman Archive/Museo Nazionale Romano, Rome.

102 A detail of a wall painting in the tomb of queen Nefertari representing the union of Ra and Isis (19th dynasty; c. 1290–1220 BCE). Werner Forman Archive/E. Strouhal.

103 A relief showing a priest of the god Ra and the goddess Hathor in the sun-temple of King Neferirkare (5th dynasty; c. 2494–2345 BCE). Werner Forman Archive/The Egyptian Museum, Cairo.

104 A relief showing the female personification of fertile estates. She offers a loaf on a mat, the hieroglyphic sign for "hetap" (offering). Werner Forman Archive/The Egyptian Museum, Cairo.

106 Detail of a tomb painting from the altar of Nefermaat at Meidum depicting a bean goose feeding (3rd–4th dynasty; c. 2680–2500 BCE). Werner Forman Archive/The Egyptian Museum, Cairo.

108 A bronze figure of a cat. Werner Forman Archive/John Kluge Collection, Virginia.

109 Bronze figure of the cat-goddess Bast (c. 600–300 BCE). Werner Forman Archive/Christie's, London.

110 A fertility figure of a woman (c. 2000–1800 BCE). Werner Forman Archive/Egyptian Museum, Berlin.

111 A detail from the tomb of Nebamun showing his wife holding a bunch of lotus flowers (18th dynasty; c. 1550–1295 BCE). Werner Forman Archive/British Museum, London.

113 Fragment of a wall painting; each woman wears a cone of unguent in her wig, which would release perfume as if melted (18th dynasty; c. 1500 BCE). Werner Forman Archive/Egyptian Museum, Berlin.

115 Relief from the demolished chapel of Hatshepsut, depicting Hatshepsut and Amun (18th dynasty; c. 1550–1295 BCE). Werner Forman Archive.

117 A detail of a wall painting from the tomb of Nebamun depicting women guests at a banquet (18th dynasty; c. 1550–1259 BCE). Werner Forman Archive/The British Museum, London.

119 A detail of a wall painting in the tomb of Pere depicting the tomb owner, and his wife before an alter laden with offerings (18th dynasty; c. 1550–1295 BCE). Werner Forman Archive/E. Strouhal.

120 Ivory clapper in the form of a hand. The oldest known forms of musical instrument in Egypt, pairs of clappers were used to accompany dances. Werner Forman Archive/private collection.

121 Part of a banquet scene from the tomb of Nabamun; one women plays the double flute while the others clap their hands (18th dynasty; c. 1550–1295 BCE). Werner Forman Archive/The British Museum, London.

123 Mummy mask of Tuya, mother of Queen Tiye and grandmother of Akhenaten. Werner Forman Archive/The Egyptian Museum, Cairo.

124 The unfinished head of Nefertiti, wife of

Akhenaton (c. 1373–1357 BCE). Werner Forman Archive/The Egyptian Museum, Cairo.

126 Relief showing servant women squeezing lilies in a press to extract the oil for use in perfume (26th dynasty; 644–525 BCE). Werner Forman Archive/Musee du Louvre, Paris.

129 As for p 2.

130 Fragment of an Amarna head (c. 1373–1357 BCE). Werner Forman Archive/Metropolitan Museum of Art, New York.

132 A detail of a wall painting of the tomb of Amen-hor-Khepeshef. The son of Ramesses III stands beside the pharaoh (20th dynasty; c. 1190–1160 BCE). Werner Forman Archive/E. Strouhal.

133 A sculpture of the relief from the temple of Queen Hatshepsut Dier el-Bahri (18th dynasty; c. 1550–1295 BCE). Werner Forman Archive.

135 A detail of a wall painting in the tomb of Khaemwaset, a son of Ramesses III, depicting a lion-headed spirit or divine being (20th dynasty; c. 1184–1153 BCE). Werner Forman Archive/E. Strouhal.

137 Detail of a painting showing Nefertiti kissing her daughter, perhaps Merytaten, under the rays of Aten (18th dynasty; c. 1552–1356 BCE). Werner Forman Archive/Brooklyn Museum, New York.

139 Detail of a relief depicting a musician, originally from the temple of Hatshepsut (18th dynasty; c. 1475–1468 BCE). Werner Forman Archive.

143 The gold fish amulet, or nekhau, was worn in the hair of young women to protect them from drowning. Werner Forman Archive/The Royal Scottish Museum, Edinburgh.

144 Detail from a wall painting in the tomb of Queen Nefertari depicts Osiris, god of the underworld, in his green form as god of fertility (19th dynasty; c. 1290–1220 BCE). Werner Forman Archive.

147 Detail from image shown on p. 11.

148 Wall painting from tomb of Tuthankhamun in which Tuthankhamun takes leave of his wife Ankhesenaumn (18th dynasty; c. 1357–1349 BCE). Werner Forman Archive/E. Strouhal.

150 Fragment of a statue from Hatshepsut's temple at Deir el-Bahari representing the queen in the form of Osiris (18th dynasty; 1490–1470 BCE). Werner Forman Archive/The Egyptian Museum, Cairo.

153 A vignette from The Book of the Dead of Neferrenpet shows the Sun-god Ra in his dawn appearance with the head of a falcon (19th dynasty; c. 1295–1186 BCE). Werner Forman Archive/Musees Royaux du Cinquantenaire, Brussels.

154 Detail from image shown on p. 144.

157 A painting in the tomb of Sennedjem. A priest leans over a mummy to perform the ritual of Osiris prior to burial (19th dynasty; c. 1295–1186 BCE). Werner Forman Archive/E. Strouhal.

158 Ba amulet from the tomb of Prince Hornakht, son of Osorkon II, found on the body of the prince, to ensure the reunion of body and soul (22nd dynasty; 874–850 BCE). Werner Forman Archive/The Egyptian Museum, Cairo.

Glossary of Names

AB *[Arb]* The heart, in which human consciousness resided.

AMUN *[A-moon]* The last of the eight frogs to be created by Ra, believed to be part of him that represented his soul.

ANUBIS *[Ah-new-bis]* God of funerary rituals and mummification. The son of Nephthys and Osiris.

APEP *[Ay-pep, Ahpep]* The snake in the seventh hour of night who ritually tries to consume the boat of Ra. Also thought to represent the ka of Set.

ATUM-RA *[A-toom Rah]* The form of Ra as a child when he emerged from Nun.

BA *[Bar]* One's identity or character that, with the ka, was thought to live on in the afterlife.

BAST *[With short "a"]* Cat-goddess of protection, healing, and love.

DJED *[Dee-jed]* The Pillar of Osiris. A column-shaped amulet evoking the power of Osiris that represents his spine.

EYE OF HORUS Popular protective amulet also known as the Eye of Ra, which depicts a stylized eye.

GEB *[With short "e"]* A god of the earth, also of fertility.

HATHOR *[With short "a", Hath-or]* The goddess of healing and love, protector of cemeteries. A sky goddess, also wife of Horus.

HEKA *[short "e", as in He-kka]* The art of spell casting.

HORUS *[Hoar-us, Horace]* Child of Isis and Osiris.

IMHOTEP *[Im-ho-tep]* An architect and high priest of Ptah who was regarded as a god of knowledge and healing some 2,000 years after his death.

ISIS *[Eye-sis]*. Goddess of magic, healing, and protection. Wife and sister of Osiris, sister to Nephthys and Set, and mother to Horus.

KA *[Car]* The astral body of a person that survived the death of the physical body.

KEPHERA *[Kef-er-a]* The scarab beetle, the form of which Ra took to create the universe.

KHAIBIT *[Car-bit]* The ghost of the self.

KHAT *[Cat]* The physical body, one of seven components of a human being that included the *ka, ba, khaibit, ren, ab,* and *sahu.*

KHNUM *[K-num]* The ram-headed god of creation, associated with Ra.

KHONSU *[Kon-soo]* The moon god and also god of war.

KHU The *sahu.*

MAAT The goddess of justice and order of the seasons.

MIN God of sex and fertility.

NUN The primordial swamp from which Ra was born from the center of a lotus flower. Also a god.

NUT *[Noot]* Mother of Isis, goddess of the sky, partner of Shu.

NEPHTHYS *[Nef-this]* Sister of Isis, a funerary goddess. Wife of Seth, mother of Anubis via Osiris.

OSIRIS *[Os-eye-ris]* Husband and brother of Isis. Lord of the underworld.

PTAH *[Tar]* God of architecture who in mythology built the palace at Heliopolis that housed the company of Ra in mortal form.

RA *[Rar]* Also written as Re. The creator-god of the universe symbolized by a sun disk.

REN A person's true name, which was necessary for the deceased's survival in the afterlife.

SAHU *[Saar-hoo]* The soul, and possibly a term for all seven components of a human being (see *khat*).

SEKHMET *[Seck-met]* The lioness goddess of **MEMPHIS**. Sister to Isis and wife of Ptah.

SELKET *[Sell-ket]* The scorpion goddess.

SHU *[Shoo]* The god of air. Consort of Tefnut.

TEFNUT *[Tef-noot, Tefnut]* The goddess of moisture.

THOTH *[or Toth, both with short "o"]* The god of writing, time, wisdom, and hidden magic.

TYET *[Tee-et]* The Knot of Isis, an amulet evoking Isis' fertility.

WADJET *[Wa-jet]* The Eye of Horus, also known as the eye of Ra. Also the cobra-goddess who protected Horus as a child.

DEDICATION

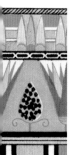

THESE ARE THE WORDS OF
ISIS, QUEEN OF MAGIC AND
OF ALL EGYPT.

I BEGIN AND END with magic, for it is all of me. Perhaps too there is love, and loyalty. There is nothing else, yet, as you will see it is enough.

I was created by Divine magic; I was adored by means of the High magic of shaven-headed priests; and shadowed by Low magic, the practice of spell-casting known as Heka.

DIVINE MAGIC IS THAT OF THE GODS.

High magic is temple-magic, that of priests. These wise folk make invocations, prayers, and offerings to the gods to ensure the health and prosperity of the country and its embodiment supreme, the pharaoh. Complex rituals and the calculations of the heavenly bodies – the stars and planets – may also be their preferment.

Then there is the art of Magical Numbers, which is also High magic. For the universe has its mystic numbers that are a secret name, a hidden code for its meaning.

Then there is architecture and engineering. Such as the pyramid-builders, who imbue their awesome creations with mystical power and meaning to stand the test of time.

8

Low magic. This art is not practiced by a priest, architect or mathematician. Every outlander believes that every Egyptian has knowledge of the cunning arts of Heka.

My unending life has mirrored the highs and lows of the magic that I practiced and the spells that have been woven for me. I have felt the ecstatic pleasure of divine love; the bliss returned when I gave healing; and the rejection that only a beggar knows. I have been a goddess enthroned in luxury in the royal city of Heliopolis; wife to a pharaoh-god, Osiris, and queen of the Two Lands of Egypt; and a fragile mortal, outcast and alone, desperately protecting my child the golden Horus.

So whence comes my reputation as the all-powerful one? For the oddities that I claim as family may be said to wield mighty power too. My brother Set near destroyed my son and me; my aunt Bast holds the secrets of ferocious love and healing; my husband Osiris is ruler of the afterlife and weighs the hearts of men in his two hands. And uncle Thoth the Wise, who measures time and rules hidden magic, caused my birth (though not as mate to my mother, as you will see). In truth, my prowess as magician is celebrated so because I am the only deity to hold the supreme power of creation itself, that which is shared with my great father, sun-god Ra. I stole this power from him, but that is another matter, later told. For now, let it be decreed that I am well placed to lend wise counsel in this, my sorcerous memoir.

My spells within this book are to be used with judgment, as even the smallest ritual can wreak mighty changes with unforeseen complication. For there is a magic in every simple thing; the writing of a name, the making of a statue, the painting of the eyes with kohl, the carrying of an amulet, all have mystic meaning that has the potential to change the very fabric of the universe.

You will remember my gratitude to my divine relation, deity of words, for giving me life; here I return it by recounting my story so that many may take it to their hearts, wherein lies the true seat of the soul.

Before I begin I will use a little magic of my own and invoke my favored uncle the thrice-great Thoth, to whom I dedicate this tome should it ever be discovered in far times to come (as my foresight tells me that it surely will). It is a simple spell that all writers can use, to ask for the divine blessing of the god of wisdom, of letters, of time, which is of great import when tiring of all words and wanting to tell the story by mouth and magic.

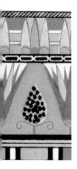

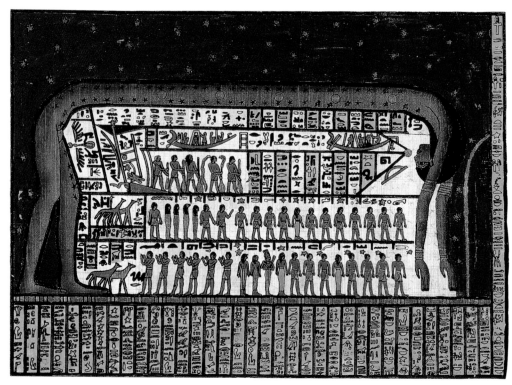

SPELL FOR REQUESTING A WATER-POT AND A PALETTE

O you great one who see your father, keeper of the book of Thoth
I have become as a spirit, besouled, mighty and equipped with the writings of Thoth.
Bring me the messenger of the earth-god who is with Set,
Bring me a water-pot and palette from the writing-kit of Thoth and the mysteries which are in them.
See, I am a scribe; bring me the corruption of Osiris
That I may write with it and that I may do what the great and good god says every day,
Being the good which you have decreed for me, O Horus of the horizon.
I will do what is right and I will send blessings to Ra daily.

READ NOW AND YOU WILL LEARN OF MANY WONDERFUL THINGS; MAKE USE OF MY LESSONS WITH WISDOM.

1 The Spell of Thoth and How it Gave Me Life

In which is it told of marshes and frogs, of a marvellous lotus and the origin of father Ra and of the universe of gods, of the mating of elements and the ordering of things. Also of Ra's curse and how the cunning of Thoth and the folly of the moon-god undid this wickedness with a game of dice.

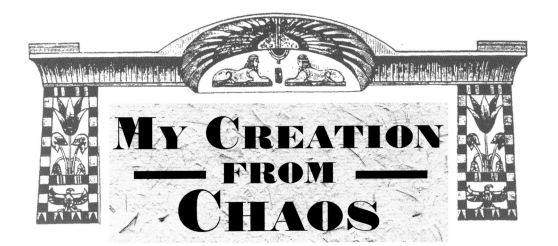

My Creation
— from —
Chaos

THIS IS MY TALE OF HOW I CAME TO BE,
AND OF MY STRANGE HISTORY.

IN A TIME before my conception and that of the universe, there was but chaos; a watery void without form or structure from which my family were to emerge. All the elements of life mingled together in a great dark marsh, and so it was for uncounted aeons. This primordial vastness was called Nun, for even before he was brought into existence as a god, he existed as the potentiality of all things.

And from the alchemy of the waters rose a lotus tall and strong, its petals bountiful, its stem straight and filled with life. From its roots emerged eight frogs who croaked and sang in unison as the bud opened to reveal the great god Ra, my grandfather, in his first and original form of Atum who manifested as a beautiful child seated at the heart of the flower. With his appearance the universe was flooded with light for the very first time.

Again the eight frogs sang and with his first words Atum-Ra named them and thus divided the elements. Hehu and Hehut were the first, for these had the nature of fire and life. Kekui and Kekuit were next for these were darkness, and close by them were Kerh and Kerhet who were the forces of night and chaos. The final pair took the nature of Ra himself. The first was Nun who was the primordial force, which had given Atum-Ra his existence. For this reason, Nun is the parent of the great sun-god even though it was Atum-Ra who gave him form and named him. Some say that Amun was the last of the divine frogs to be named for he was part of the soul of Ra, that which is hidden from the eyes of gods and men. Later he took upon himself many other shapes, for it is in this aspect that Ra later ruled supreme. It is from Amun that the beautiful, mysterious, round-faced moon was born, and he was named Khonsu, a vain god who shall figure later in my story.

Now heaven did not exist and the earth had not yet come into being, so when the child Atum wished to step down from the lotus there was nothing upon which he could set his feet, so Atum-Ra took upon himself the form of Khepera the scarab-beetle. He worked the greatest spell that there has ever been upon his own heart, granting himself the powers of creation itself for Khepera knew that this was right, and this rightness too was given spiritual form as the goddess Maat who is justice and honor and correct thought and behavior.

I now know something of this potent spell. For Ra, speaking his secret name that no divine god or mortal may know, thus created my universe. I confess this is how I came to have the power of creation, and take the mantle of queen of magic; yet all this is to come and be sure that I will reveal it all.

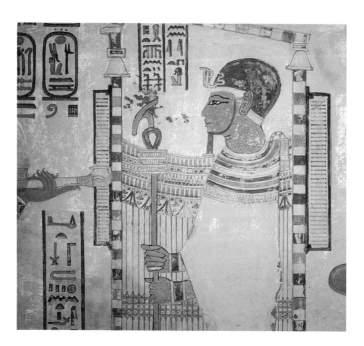

THE SCARAB

The scarab is the most common of Ancient Egyptian amulets. The sculpted form of the beetle can still be found in great numbers in the deserts surrounding the fertile Nile valley. It is one of the most potent aspects of the sun god, Ra. Many prayers and incantations were addressed to Ra in his form of Khepera. The scarab Khepera is also called "the keeper of the name" and it is in this form that the sun god closely guards his secret name, the word of power that caused the universe itself to come into being (see pages 14–16). As an extension of this idea, it became the custom for Egyptians to have their names inscribed on the underside of a scarab which would then be worn, usually on a string around the neck. As most Egyptian peasants were illiterate, they could use their scarab to stamp their signature on a scribes' clay tablet without having to grasp a stylus.

Every word that the scarab Khepera now spoke created something new, for in the manner of the scarab, Khepera molded the universe from the watery matter about him and gave it life. Then returning to the shape of Atum, Ra took his manhood in his hand and emitted two further gods from his semen which lay upon the marsh. These were Shu who is air, and Tefnut who is moisture. Then seeing the beauty of all that he had done Atum-Ra-Khepera wept and from his tears were born reptiles and all manner of creeping things, then animals, fish and birds, until at last men and women came into being. Though some say that Ra now manifested all his forms, filling creation with light and life, and it was as his essence or *khu* that he took the form of ram-headed Khnum and made the bodies of men and women upon a potter's wheel.

As the manifestations of Ra continued, his very voice became personified as the god Thoth, the measurer of time. He became my beloved teacher and mentor and it is he who is responsible for my birth although he is not my father.

ALL WILL BE TOLD IN ITS PROPER PLACE.

As Ra was creator and king, so Thoth soon became his vizier and first minister. It was in the mighty, magical name of Ra that Thoth then commanded all that was to be done. It was he who regulated the seasons and he who numbered the days. It was Thoth, disguised as a baboon, who invented the art of writing, and it was he who became the first master of the magic arts and my teacher as will be told. So great was the sagacity of Thoth was that he soon found a kinship of spirit with ostrich-feathered Maat, who is justice and order. The two thus became husband and wife and knew divine love. It is my opinion that it is because of this love that I, my sister, and my brothers now exist.

The tasks of creation were then taken over by Ptah, divine architect and personification of the face of Ra, and ram-headed Khnum. Ptah, bald headed and swathed in mummy wrappings, formed the solid beneath and the vaporous above, while Khnum, still seated at his potter's wheel, formed all the animals and birds that live between them. Thus was Khnum regarded as the source of life and was worshipped at the headwaters of the sacred Nile. Although it must be said that poor Khnum was soon exhausted by his efforts of molding the physical bodies of each and every living creature and was at his wit's end. Then Thoth (ever wise) suggested that he include a miniature potter's wheel in the bellies of each female creature so that they could reproduce themselves without Khnum going to the trouble of completing this onerous task for them.

It was this innovation that displeased Ra and began a galaxy of troubles. Perhaps the wisdom of Thoth was lacking in this instance, or could it be that he was further sighted than anyone could have suspected.

The first hint of a problem began with the two first created offspring of Ra, Shu and Tefnut. They had not been idle in all this time for they found the powerful lure of physical lust and, following the dictates of nature had mingled their bodies together and produced children of their own. These were Geb, god of the solid earth and Nut, goddess of the sky. Of these two, the goddess Nut was the more willful for it is said that she tore herself from her mother's womb, so impatient was she to be part of creation.

Such was the impetuosity of my mother.

These two in turn grew amorous but Ra was angered, for he too had cast lustful eyes upon my mother, and set their father Shu between them to keep the lovers apart. Such was the jealousy of Ra that he had my parents forever divided. Shu, divine god of the air, had poor Geb trodden down to become all the lands of the world, the contours of his body forming hills, valleys, mountain ranges, deserts and fertile pastures. Nut was sent soaring upward to cover the sky, where she became the deity of the firmament who provides rain. With the tips of her fingers supporting her arched body in the east, and the tips of her toes in the west, she remains above us still, the myriads of stars speckling her body. Some say that Nut was transformed into a celestial cow, and it is in this shape that she arches over the world. It is also said that each evening as Ra assumes the form of Atum as the setting sun, that Nut swallows him whole and that he spends the night within her body only to be born as Khepera from her womb in the morning. Thus is Nut sometimes thought to be the mother of Ra. Even if this is so, Ra's jealousy remained for he had set his heart against the love of Geb and Nut and cursed Nut saying that even though Geb had filled her womb with life she would be unable to bear children upon any day or night of the year.

A Spell For Separation

In memory of my parents do I dedicate this spell. Their separation, forming the earth and the air, is the very canvas upon which my story as mortal queen is played. I do suspect mortals use this ritual to end love when two must part. Of wax, or with ink, the form of my father, earth-god Geb, is made. And this incantation is spoken.

THE TEMPLE AT KARNAK

Built over the reigns of many dynasties of pharaohs, Karnak was the largest religious building in the world, and has been a pilgrimage site for around 4,000 years, from its inception to present-day tourism. The complex comprises the Sacred Enclosure of Amun, or great temple of the sun-god Ra, along with a sacred lake and a scattering of smaller temples. Its largest area, however, is the Hypostyle Hall, which measures 54,000 square feet. The hall was begun during the reign of King Sety I (c.1290–1279 BCE) and completed by his son, Ramesses II (c. 1279–1213 BCE).

The cosmic creativity of Ra was celebrated by the performance of a time-traveling ritual by Karnak priests. This aspect of the sun-god was represented in the form of the Atum-Ra statue, in the Sacred Enclosure of Atum. Beginning at the outer boundary of the temple, the priests in procession would step backward toward the statue situated at its center. The ritual symbolized a backward journey through time, from the edge of civilization to the great creator, Atum-Ra, at the beginning of the universe. It is known that Ramesses II also practiced this ritual, which acknowledged his connection to the divinity of the gods and, as pharaoh, his role as sole interpreter of their wishes on earth.

OH FLAME OF WOE!
The father of Geb curses Geb in his heart
And so, the mountains and very earth are fired with the torment of
  Geb.
Let the fury of every god and goddess be cast upon ____ and ____
  (mortals do use their two names here)
And anger shall pierce their hearts, even while they sleep.
Quarrel strikes at love until love surrenders
And forever will they disagree.

THE CURSE OF RA

MY MOTHER, NUT, cursed by Ra never to bring forth her divine children on any day of the year, was condemned to perpetual labor. Such was Nut's torment that her cries coursed the heavens, and all gods knew her cruel pain.

Now, as if in reaction to the senseless anger of the sun-god, in true wisdom Thoth, the god of measurement, thought long and deep on the matter.

The solution to the problem came about in this way. Thoth was so wise that he knew that great benefit would come from the gifts of the children of Nut and Geb so cruelly separated by Ra's implacable will. So, mindful of Nut's agony, Thoth transformed himself into a playful baboon and went to Khonsu, the moon, beguiling the lamp of night, with his antics. As the serene moon-boat dipped in the West the baboon nimbly leapt aboard and sailed with Khonsu through the depths of the underworld.

It was at this time that he made Khonsu marvel at the way he could make sounds and words into pictures, and thus did Thoth reveal the art of writing. Now fascinated, Khonsu promised the baboon that he would grant him any boon he desired if only he would teach the moon this wonderful magic. Thoth, ever cunning, said that he wished only to play, and feigning frivolity challenged Khonsu to a game of dice. Laughing delightedly Khonsu assented and the two, moon-god and baboon, sat down to play.

At first Khonsu rolled the higher scores and the baboon jumped up and down, complimenting the round-faced god on his skill. Khonsu for his part has ever loved flattery and was thus happy to agree when the baboon-Thoth suggested a small wager, just to make the game more interesting.

At first, no more than fruits and shells were wagered on the outcome of each roll of the dice. And these games were invariably won by the moon-god. At length the baboon hinted that the bets should be for something of more value; Khonsu again agreed, and this time they played for gold and silver. And so it went on, day upon day, month upon month, for almost a full year. Do not forget that through all this time my sky-mother Nut still groaned in the agony of her perpetual labor.

As the game progressed the stakes grew higher still, until at last the baboon-Thoth suggested that they wager for a measure of the moon's own light. To this bold plan Khonsu grew thoughtful while doubts assailed him, but with more artful flattery the baboon eventually prevailed upon vain Khonsu to agree. So saying, Khonsu threw the dice again.

THE ENCHANTMENT OF THE DICE

BONES, BONES roll as you may
Your numbers choose both night and day
Where the power of sky and stars hold sway
To cause these bones to roll my way
Roll for me this day.

THOTH THEN BLEW UPON THE DICE AND AS YOU WILL SEE, MY FUTURE WAS FOREVER CAST.

CASTING THE BONES

The earliest six-sided dice were made of baked clay, excavated from a site in Mesopotamia, northern Iraq, in c. 2750 BCE. In Egypt, dice have been recovered from sites dating to 1320 BCE. The Victorian Egyptologist, Flinders Petrie, discovered a stone die with markings in Naucratis, Egypt, which he dated to 600 BCE.

Finds at sites pre-1320 BCE, however, have revealed sets of animal bones thought to have been used as dice – which does reflect the "bones" referred to, rather than literally "die" or "dice" in Thoth's enchantment spell. Known as tali (Latin) or astragali (Greek), the bones came from the heel of hoofed animals such as goats, deer, and sheep. Each bone had four flat faces and two rounded ends, but each side looked different so that they were easy to distinguish when they were thrown during a game. Naturally, they formed pairs.

Greek and Roman games of chance were played with four astragali, which were numbered. The lowest throw, known as "the dogs," resulted when all ones were thrown – which may account for the saying "Going to the dogs." The highest was known as the Venus throw, when four different sides came up.

But this time fortune was with Thoth, admittedly because he used a muttered spell to improve his chances. Unheard by Khonsu, Thoth whispered this incantation to the dice. The throws of the baboon's dice were now invariably higher than those of Khonsu. The scowling moon-god now knew defeat over and over again and groaning, he surrendered a portion of his beloved light each time. Soon his full rounded face became a little thinner but they played on, Khonsu confident that the next throw would see a change to his fortunes.

IT WAS NOT TO BE.

Little by little, the wily Thoth gathered enough light to create five extra days. These, as the measurer of time, he added to the end of the year that Ra had decreed. Laughing, the baboon made a stately bow and swiftly took his leave of the furious Khonsu by leaping from the moon boat and transforming himself into an ibis bird as he fell. His wings caught the wind and, with the newly won light safely carried upon his head, Thoth sped heavenward.

Thus does the moon wax and wane for there is not light enough in that orb for Khonsu to remain at his fullness at all times. It is as a remembrance of this victory that clever Thoth bears the crescent horns of the moon upon his head whether he appears in the guise of an ibis bird or as a baboon.

THE EGYPTIAN CALENDAR

The civil calendar of 360 days was divided into three seasons, each comprising four months with thirty days in each. These seasons followed the cycles of the Nile. The year began when the star Sirius (which the Egyptians knew as "Sothis") rose over the horizon with Ra, the sun; this synchronicity heralded the annual flooding of the Nile (known as Inundation, or akhet), ensuring the fertility of crops. Sirius is also a symbol of Isis, believed to be the brightest star in the galaxy. It is part of the Canis Major constellation and is found near Orion; it was given its alternative name, the dog-star, because celestial pattern resembles the nose of a dog. Inundation, which lasted from June 21 to October 21, was followed by Emergence (proyet) (October 21–February 21) and Summer, or shomu (February 21–June 21) so completing the Egyptian year.

It is well attested that the priests of Ancient Egypt knew that their 360-day calculation of the length of the year was inaccurate. The five extra days stolen by Thoth were added to the beginning of the new year, when Sirius-Isis and Ra were visible together, and these days were set aside for feasting to celebrate the cosmic arrival of the goddess. The myth of the cheating of the moon-god also cleverly explains how the calendar was rectified without challenging the ultimate power of Ra and the system of belief this engendered. The curse of the sun-god was not broken, but ingeniously circumvented by the cunning of Thoth.

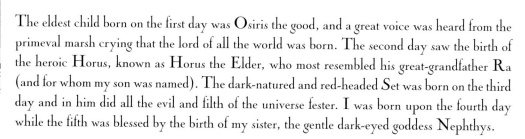

Tarrying no longer, Thoth made haste to assist at the birth of the children of Geb and Nut. To help he called Tauret the hippopotamus-goddess and ugly Bes, the kindly and merry dwarf-jester of Ra. Thus it was that the curse of the all-father was undone and Nut was relieved of her agony by bearing no less than five children, one upon each of the extra days that Thoth had cunningly won for her. As each child emerged into the universe, Thoth bestowed the name that child would bear so that they would be counted among the company of the gods.

The eldest child born on the first day was Osiris the good, and a great voice was heard from the primeval marsh crying that the lord of all the world was born. The second day saw the birth of the heroic Horus, known as Horus the Elder, who most resembled his great-grandfather Ra (and for whom my son was named). The dark-natured and red-headed Set was born on the third day and in him did all the evil and filth of the universe fester. I was born upon the fourth day while the fifth was blessed by the birth of my sister, the gentle dark-eyed goddess Nephthys.

When all these things were accomplished and heaven, earth, sea, and sky were in their proper place. And all the creatures that were lived according to their natures and all the gods that maintained them were at their stations, that Ra, greatest and first of all the deities, grew weary of eternity and gazed with envy upon the impermanence and excitement of the world of mortal men.

So there is the beginning of my tale, as it was recounted to me by Thoth himself. I have not told of the magic of the true name of Ra and how it was this that brought all things into being. Nor have I told of the great and terrible Book of Thoth in which my mentor set down all he knew of the mysteries of the universe, but I will tell all that I may.

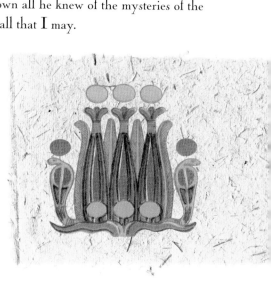

2 WHAT MY GREAT FATHER RA TAUGHT ME

IN WHICH IT IS TOLD OF THE FOLLY
AND DESIRE OF THE DIVINE RA,
OF EARTHLY LIFE AND CITY
BUILDING. ALSO, OF HIS INFIRMITY
AND THE MOCKERY OF MEN.
AND OF HOW RA TOOK HIS DREADFUL
REVENGE, AS WELL AS
A LESSON IN MIRROR MAGIC AND
SELF-PROTECTION.
AND FINALLY OF HOW MANKIND
SAVED THE GODS BY DROWNING
BLOOD-LUST IN BEER.

OF LOVE
— AND —
JEALOUSY

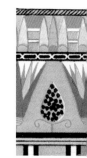

IT IS TIME TO TELL OF HOW I, ISIS CAME TO
DWELL UPON THE EARTH THOUGH TRUTH TO
TELL IT WAS NOT BY MY WILL OR MY
INCLINATION. IN THE FIRST DAYS, IN THE PLACE
OF ETERNITY I HAD BUT LITTLE WILL. NOR DID
I OR MY BROTHERS AND SISTER HAVE ANY
ABILITY TO CHOOSE FOR OURSELVES IN
ANY MANNER.

WE FIVE CHILDREN of Geb and Nut existed in the opulence of the palace of Ra, the great father of the sun and all creation. Though it seemed to us more of a prison. Immortal, imperishable and beautiful, we could not appreciate the very marvel of our being and cursed great Ra for his tyranny and apparent neglect of us. What did we know of suffering or toil? It seems now that we gazed outward into the universe of change from a gorgeous place of changelessness.

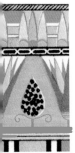

Yet it must be said that Ra did, on occasion seem to take a special interest in me, although he maintained his distance from my siblings. Sometimes I would feel his fiery gaze upon me and when I dared to raise my eyes to his, I will swear that I saw puzzlement within those piercing, golden hawk-like orbs. Maybe it was because of my semblance to Nut, my wilful mother of the sky, who had so inflamed Ra's jealous heart with her lust for my father.

Or so I once thought.

Our aloof grandfather Ra, mightiest of all the gods, was possessed of a restless heart. From his vantage point of eternity, his Sun-Boat of a Million Years, this greatest of deities brooded on all the life that had sprung from him. All things were of his own nature, yet he remained separate from them. He daily traversed the heavens gazing down upon a work of vast accomplishment yet he saw it all from afar, observing the flight of birds far below, the movements of animals and the toiling of men. He watched the flow of the terrestrial Nile, the ebb and flow of passing time. He saw birth and death, joy and sorrow without comprehending all that he observed and was deeply saddened by the remoteness of his soul.

In time Ra, the first father, the self-created progenitor of all came to a far-reaching conclusion, which was this: if he was to understand all that he had created from his lonely tears then he must of necessity enter into his own creation. Becoming a mortal being like his human worshippers, he would thus come to know them better. Such was the will of my grandfather.

My kind mentor the wise Thoth, most sagacious of gods who travelled with the great one recording all that transpired on earth, was fiercely opposed to mighty Ra's resolution and strongly advised against the supreme one leaving the celestial eternity and entering into mundane time. The Ibis-headed measurer of things was not alone in his deep misgivings.

My father Geb, now thrust down to earth, still angry that he had been forcibly parted from his beloved mate, my mother Nut, did not want to bear the weight of his hated parent Ra. My mother Nut (both mysteriously daughter and mother of the sun-god), banished to the sky to bear Ra's sky-boat through the firmament, could not see why Ra should leave the heavens when she could not.

Great Ra would not be swayed and by magic prepared a mortal body or khat for his ka to inhabit. For it is a truth that gods and men alike have no less than seven selves and so it has been from the beginning. Herein lies a mystery, that of life and death, of animation, breath and soul, of shadow and of substance, but to understand this one must possess the secret name of the great god as I, the once despised Isis, do.

FOLLOW CLOSELY FOR THIS IS PART OF THE TALE OF HOW I GAINED THIS BOON.

SEVENTH HEAVEN

The Egyptians believed that the body had seven components. Each of these had its own funerary rites, hence the widespread practice of mummification as well as the preservation of various organs of the body, and the establishment of fetishes or cult statues to house the more incorporeal selves.

The first of these selves, the khat, described the physical form. The second self, or ka, was cognate with the astral body or etheric double, the energy-body that exists outside the physical body. The ba , the third self, was usually pictured in hieroglyphic writings as a bird possessed of a human head. It can be thought of as one's intrinsic character, as an animal spirit-guide that symbolizes our deepest instincts. The ba and ka were thought to survive into the afterlife.

The fourth self is the khaibit, the ghost of the self, identified with the shadow thrown by strong light; the fifth self is the ren, one's true name. Pharaohs who had posthumously fallen from favor had their names obliterated from temples and other public places. This would condemn their souls to oblivion, because it would also result in the destruction of all the other selves. The ren was therefore a necessary ingredient for the survival of death.

The Egyptians believed that consciousness resided in the human heart, or ab, the sixth self. The Egyptian Book of the Dead details the ceremony of the weighing of the heart against the feather of truth, or maat, in order to be admitted to the afterlife.

The seventh self is the sahu or soul, but this may also refer to the seven selves in total. This mysterious seventh portion is also called the shu. Shu is also the name of Isis' grandfather, deity of the air, and one of the sons of Ra. In this context, shu is thought to represent breath, which may link with the funerary rite of opening the mouth of the deceased in order to release the shu. The third word used for the seventh self is khu, or spirit. This description is used in the sense of "blessed one" or "one who has ascended. "

HOW BEAUTY BECAME — ME —

NOW **I** CAN TELL OF OUR SECOND BIRTH WHEN
I, MY SIBLINGS, AND GREAT FATHER **R**A,
DESCENDED TO EARTH.

SURELY **R**A WITH ALL HIS DIVINE FORESIGHT could have foreseen what was to happen. Surely he of all beings could have prevented the horror that was to come. If he did, then he chose not to prevent it and thus persisted in fulfilling his misguided plan. Or do I judge him too harshly? Can it be that I still resent the being who tried to prevent the birth of both myself and that of my beloved Osiris?

Perhaps Ra himself knew fear or trepidation, because when the moment came for him to assume human form he could not bear to make the descent alone. Eight of us, his relatives, were commanded to join him. Among these were myself, my beloved Osiris, and my dark-complexioned sister, Nephthys; Horus (my brother, rather than my son who was to be named for him) and Set the guileful. I will pause a moment because I cannot even think of him without hate clouding my heart. But enough; it suffices to say that just as Ra incarnated in a corporeal body, we too were forced into fleshly form. Can it be that this was the first time I saw my eternal love, Osiris, as others imagined him to be? Oh it seemed to me that the radiance of his smile outshone even the glory of the newly embodied Ra.

ANNU, THE CITY OF THE PHOENIX

The city of Annu, or On, is commonly known by its Greek name of Heliopolis. From prehistoric times this conurbation was the religious center of Lower Egypt, although now it exists as a suburb of the metropolis of Cairo. In addition to its religious importance as the cult-center of Ra in his form as Atum, the first-created (see page 13) and of Ptah, the divine architect, Heliopolis often served as the political hub of Egypt and residence of the Pharaohs. According to the Greek writer Heroditus, Heliopolis was the destination of the phoenix. Once every thousand years the creature would fly to the city from its home in Arabia, there to build its own funeral pyre. The kindling, ignited by the rays of the sun, would consume the body of the bird. However, the smoldering ashes would work a powerful magic, and miraculously the renewed Phoenix would rise from them to live again. This legend may be a dim reflection of the events of the earthly rule of the sun-god Ra, for as Isis says he too grew old and risked mortal death, far from the safety of his cosmic home.

Even in our corporeal state it was unthinkable that Ra could be anything other than king. So we, his once-despised descendants, assumed the roles of his earthly court and made our home where we first set foot upon the earth. And how was it that mankind served us so willingly, you ask? To answer that I must forget all modesty and proclaim that our subjects worshipped us immediately, recognizing our might and beauty as divine in nature. They had known no gods before us and truly, we had never conceived of making ourselves known to them in this way. All this now changed with the commencement of our paradise on earth. By the command of King Ra, the construction of the holy city of Annu was begun.

It was as the work commenced that I heard Grandfather Ra speak a spell to ensure the safety of his new home. The words are set out thus, and I have written them carefully from my memory here.

It was natural that in the course of the old man's ageing that he often hawked and spat and I, esteeming every part of my grandfather holy, collected some of his spittle and preserved it in a small stoppered jar. Even though at that time I knew but little of high magic nor the more humble arts of Heka, there must have been some instinct stirring in my breast that this fluid possessed a mighty power that I could call upon when necessity demanded it.

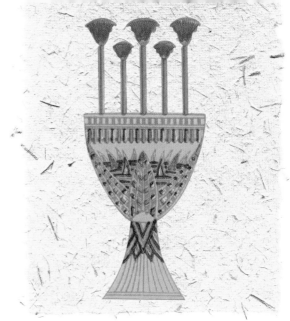

I KEPT THIS FIRST LITTLE AMULET SECRET FROM ALL OTHERS, EVEN MY BELOVED OSIRIS.

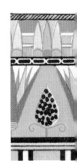

It may seem strange but even though Ra was now very frail, he still possessed the power of creation within his crumbling frame. From him emanated the powers that order time and the world; it was by his high will that the sun rose and set, the Nile flooded in due season and that the earth was fruitful. Only thus could his people be content with his rule. But Ra, now ruled by time, suffered so that even his own creation was prone to forgetfulness. At length the days and seasons became confused. Endless nights followed days of drought; the rain that purified and fed the earth came but little, so crops withered and dust choked the Two Lands like the wrappings of death. All was the dream and the creation of Ra and that dream had become a nightmare for all of us who dwelt within it. The people cried out for mercy and begged the gods for deliverance. In vain did we, the company of Heliopolis, beseech our grandfather to either return to the heavens or to grant his power to another so that his people could be governed better. Tragically, Ra had grown rather deaf and immensely stubborn and would hear none of our entreaties.

At length the inevitable happened. The hungry people rose up and overthrew the temples of the gods. They cursed Ra and his family in their desperate hunger and swore that they would drive us all from the face of the earth. All was lost, for beyond the confines of the palace the whole earth was in turmoil. My guileful brother Set put up a spirited defence of the palace rendering the place impregnable, but barbarism ruled without and the crimes of humanity were without number. Yet I could not find it in my heart to blame the starving mortals; instead I found that the true blame lay with the intransigence of Ra, though I dared not voice my thoughts.

At last, and far too late, Ra finally paid heed to the curses and mockery of men. Bestirring himself he went by secret ways to the primordial swamp that had given him birth from the lotus that had emerged from the chaos that is called Nun. Here by deep magic did Ra invoke the spirit of that chaos, named him and gave him form. From the unplumbed depths and watery ways came this newest-named yet oldest of gods. Great Nun the uncreated one, manifested in the form of a gigantic man, green with mold and pond-scum, streaming with water and weeds, the sacred lotus which was the seed of the universe upon his godly brow.

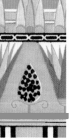

Ra spoke: "O eldest of gods, ancestor of ancestors, in my foolishness I have taken the form and nature of a mortal man and entered time to live amongst humanity who were born of the tears of my loneliness. But now these ingrates have turned against me and those gods who are my descendants. They curse my name and overthrow my temples."

WHAT SHOULD I DO?

In answer, the sonorous voice of Nun came forth: "My son, thou who named me and gave me form, mightiest of gods, greatest of kings, your throne though it seems about to topple is safe. Return now to Annu, your city and there pluck out your eye and send it forth against those who would destroy you". So saying, the great bulk of the ancient god sank down into the primeval waters of chaos.

Whether it was in body or in Ka form that Ra journeyed I cannot say, but for many days the god-king sat enthroned in his wondrous hall brooding on the words of Nun while the discordant sounds of riot reached us all.

Finally, with a resolution unsurpassed Ra reached into the socket of his right eye and with a terrible scream of agony tore forth his eye and cast it bleeding to the ground. Then a strange and terrifying magic was accomplished: a new deity was born. The eye became a ball of brilliant light and it was obvious to the assembled gods that it sought a form in keeping with its nature. It had been born of the rage of the greatest one and his anguish manifested as a huge and terrible lioness, a creature of fierce passions with a desire to avenge the sun-god's pain.

"Sekhmet the mighty do I call you," cried Ra, "and Nesert, the burning flame". Thus this new-born daughter of Ra was given a measure of the sun god's power and all of his unbounded fury. Then Ra in his pain spoke a mighty spell that may still be spoken by those who seek to avenge a wrong.

THE EYE OF RA

Several Egyptian goddesses were habitually addressed by the title "Eye of Ra". The wild and bloodthirsty Sekhmet is an obvious example yet others, the kindly Hathor and the seductive Bast, also gain this sobriquet. In addition a protective amulet commonly worn as jewelry on the chest took the form of an eye. This was called the wadjet, meaning "whole one", and is often referred to as either the "Eye of Ra" or the "Eye of Horus", both deities being solar in nature.

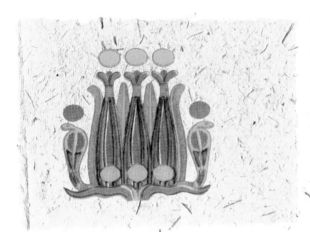

THE INCANTATION OF SEEKING VENGEANCE

My EYE HAS SEEN the offence against me.
My eye has witnessed the evil done to me.
And as my eye has seen, so then let my eye seek restitution.
As I was smitten so shall I smite.
Let the power of my eye go forth, evil for evil,
good for good, let Maat be the judge.

THIS IS A POTENT SPELL not to be spoken lightly. The power of Sekhmet is a terrifying thing to unleash. Also those that speak these words must be sure that they do not offend against justice and morality for the implacable goddess Maat, daughter of Ra, arbitrator of the universe, is the judge in this matter. If the cause not be just then the anger of Sekhmet may be returned to he who sent it out.

MAAT AND JUSTICE

The goddess Maat was the first-born daughter of Ra and wife of Thoth. She represents law and moral justice and is portrayed bearing a single ostrich feather in her headdress. Traditionally, the heart of the deceased was weighed against that of Maat's feather. If the scale was equal, the dead person could enter the afterlife. An echo of her form may be found in the blindfold figure of Justice that is perched on the dome of many courthouses around the world. Maat also embodied cosmic order as well as human justice – she was thought to regulate the proper running of the universe, the passage of the seasons, right thinking, right actions and proper social interactions. Although there are few Egyptian temples to Maat, she was of great importance. In dynastic times, the chief minister to the pharaoh was called the High Priest of Maat, and the papyrus text, The Book of the Heavenly Cow, details a particular Maat spell for truth. This ritual involved the magician painting an image of the goddess on his tongue (presumably using vegetable dye). From then on his words would be true, and become truth, for whatever he pronounced would happen in reality.

Of Blood-Lust
and
Its Dangers

THIS PART OF MY TALE TAUGHT ME THAT AN APPETITE FOR DESTRUCTION CAN COME FROM WITHIN, NOT WITHOUT. IT CAN BE AS FAMILIAR AND REPELLENT AS MY BLOODTHIRSTY SISTER-GODDESS, SEKHMET.

As MIGHTY Ra had given her instruction to destroy all, so, Sekhmet let out a ghastly roar, crying, "Flee from me O humanity, though it shall avail you not. Hide yourselves in the deserts and among the mountains and let fear triumph in your hearts; for I am Sekhmet, I am vengeance and bloody death." With that, the lioness raged through the valley of the Nile and everywhere that she met with mortals she slew them without mercy, rending their flesh and drinking greedily of their blood. Mankind reacted swiftly, taking up arms against this new terror but it was to no avail. After Sekhmet was finished there was not one man left alive to witness the carnage of her passing.

Dealing death was the delight of Sekhmet, and the more she slew, the more she fed and grew ever more powerful. Greater still did her passion for slaughter grow and as the light grew dim night after night she returned to presence of Ra, saying, "This day I have been mighty against mankind. Not one stands alive where I have been. I have waded in human blood and drunk my fill; for the joy of killing gladdens my heart and makes me hungry for more." In the morning, Sekhmet again set out, and again the day was filled with the pitiful cries of the dying.

Now terror came to the company of gods for mankind was in peril of extinction so Osiris the Good, and Shu the god of the air pleaded with Ra to end this madness. "Great Ra, surely you have reaped enough vengeance. Let your terrible daughter now rest or she will destroy all that which you have created," they said in unison. To this statement, all assembled added their voice (even wily Set, who usually so delighted in mischief) for even the lord of the desert storm was alarmed by the blood-thirst of the ferocious Sekhmet.

Ra then spoke.

"The wisdom of Osiris and the compassion of Shu shall prevail for I too have sickened of this carnage and will have no more of it. When next my daughter Sekhmet comes before me I will command her to cease." When we heard these words we rejoiced, and for the first time in a long while knew peace in our hearts.

That night, gory Sekhmet returned to the presence of her father. As was her habit she recounted the number she had slain and described the agony of their dying. Ra listened gravely and then said, "My daughter, I created you from rage and pain, but these have now passed from me and I repent of my rashness. Slay no more but settle here with me. Let mankind live in peace and multiply once more. I swear that they will worship you as a goddess, and give you great honor if only you will desist."

But Sekhmet knew nothing but fury. Compassion was not in her nature so she replied in anger, "Can it be that you are not as great as I had supposed O Ra? Does your courage fail you now that absolute victory in sight? Do the weak counsels of lesser gods sway your judgment? If all that is so then it is time you abandoned your throne and allowed another, stronger deity to rule."

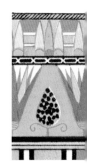

So saying, Sekhmet let out a terrifying roar and bounded from the palace crying, "For destruction was I created and thus will I destroy!"

The assembled gods were appalled at this turn of events but none, not even I had any advice to offer grandfather Ra. However, a small and limited plan did hatch in my mind. Since it now seemed that Sekhmet had abandoned all loyalty to the gods and was intent on wreaking havoc on any she encountered, I considered it prudent to put in place a ward or spell of protection to preserve both ourselves and any mortals who came to us for help. To this end I implored the thrice-great Thoth, the wisest and most knowledgeable of the gods, for his assistance. Thoth had ever been fond of me, and he gave his counsel readily.

The Mirror Charm to Repel the Evil Eye

THE SPELL OF THOTH was simple indeed and most potent. Under his direction I took a bronze hand mirror of grace and beauty and with a pin from my hair scoured the back surface until it was dull and scratched. Now the use of this trinket is twofold. When there is one whose attentions are false and whom you suspect may do you harm by envy, then it is a small matter to contrive to gaze upon their reflection in this mirror and then their true motives will soon be made plain.

If someone is actively trying to do you harm (as ferocious Sekhmet was) then it is the scoured side that is employed for the magic. The scratches on the reverse of the mirror will return the evil to the sender without delay. Remember that it was from the eye of Ra that Sekhmet took her birth and thus the effects of this evil, which may be termed as wickedness and envy, are called the Evil Eye.

The method of both of these enchantments involves an invocation to the beauteous goddess Hathor the cow-eyed and horned one.

SPEAK THE WORDS:

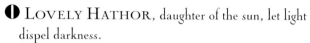

O LOVELY HATHOR, daughter of the sun, let light
   dispel darkness.
As **R**a rises in the morning let the eye of light dispel the eye
   of darkness.
Beloved goddess, hear my prayer.

When these words are spoken take care that you do not glance
at the scoured side of the mirror not even for the briefest second,
but continue to look upon your reflection in the unmarked,
shiny surface.

Let your mind dwell on the evil that has been done to you and raise the mirror toward the one
who has sent this mischief. Although if this person be not present then raise it toward the
direction where he or she dwells.

SPEAK THE WORDS:

THUS DO **I** return the evil wishes and unkindness that have been sent to me;

May Hathor be my messenger as she was messenger for **R**a.

The harm of the Evil Eye will then be returned to the wicked person who sent it to plague you.
As always it is wise to conclude your spell with a heartfelt word of thanks to the deity who has
accomplished this deed on your behalf, so speak the words:

IN GRATITUDE do **I** praise the grace of
Hathor the cow-eyed.

May her blessed favor long continue.

A pinch of fragrant incense cast into a flame as an
offering to divine Hathor would be pleasing to
her, because she has ever been fond of perfumes.

— Fury — Knows No Bounds

As the terrible deeds of Sekhmet escalated, terrible indeed was her fury. If she had raged before, she was doubly monstrous now. Indeed this dreadful episode taught me never to negotiate with those who are truly mad or inflamed, for it will come to naught.

Rivers of blood flowed, and it was Sekhmet's delight to wade in gore, lapping greedily at the blood of the slain. In desperation great Ra (the crisis having restored his clarity of mind) asked each of the gods for counsel but none could offer advice. Then spoke Ra, "If none of the gods can aid me to end this monster's ravages, I must beg humanity to help me. As it is Sekhmet, my daughter who causes this carnage, then it is to the daughters of men to whom I must turn."

By the command of Ra we gods set forth to seek out the survivors of Sekhmet's rage. Faster than the storm wind did we fly. To the mountains, the deserts and the desolate places did we go. And there in huddled pockets we found the remnants of humanity. These few we brought to Annu, there to be preserved under the protection of Ra.

Then did Ra speak once more: "You gods go now as far to the South as the isle of Elephantine at the first cataract of the bloodied Nile. There procure the roots and apples of the soporific mandrake plant and bring them here to me."

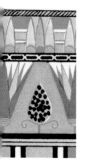

Once more we flew like the wind, far to the South where the potent mandrake grew. With haste we collected as many of the plants as we could although this was a distressing experience for the plants wailed like children when we tore them from the ground.

ONLY OUR IMMORTALITY PRESERVED US FROM THE FATAL SCREAM.

On our return to Annu we found that great Ra had not been idle. He had commanded that the womenfolk in the city set about crushing many bushels of barley; and when this not inconsiderable task was accomplished, the ever-resourceful daughters of men set to brewing no less than seven thousand jugs of strong beer.

Under the direction of mighty Ra, we gods then prepared a wonderful potion from the mandrakes which was then added to each jug, turning it a deep sanguine hue. To each was also added the juice of the pomegranate, making the liquid appear as blood. Before the dusk had dimmed the vault of heaven, great Ra commanded that these seven thousand jugs be placed before the city. Some have claimed that the liquid was poured over the land to give it an appearance of a vast lake of blood, but this is not so. I know this for I, Isis, was on hand to witness these events.

By moon-rise the war-weary Sekhmet returned to the plain before Annu. At once the heady aroma assailed her sensitive nostrils and she bent to lap at the contents of the first jug. So entrancing did she find the brew that she emptied the jar immediately and moved on to the next. Full seven thousand jugs did she drain while we the gods and mortals within the city held our breath. Then a miracle! How we all laughed with relief to see the mighty lioness reeling about drunkenly, unable to control her head and limbs. How we rejoiced when Sekhmet fell, unable to resist to potent brew we had delivered up for her pleasure. Soon, we ventured forth to view the huge body of the recumbent, snoring lioness.

Then great Ra came forth and by his secret magic arts called back to himself the hatred of Sekhmet. By his words of power Ra transformed malice into joy, anger into peace. This very cantrip may still be spoken by all those who desire harmony and the ending of feuds.

MAGICAL MANDRAKE

The mandrake or Mandragora plant derives from Greek words that approximate to "harmful to cattle"; to the Arabs, it was known as "Satan's apple." Its root was thought to resemble the trunk and limbs of a human, the place of the head being taken by foliage. Mandrake fruit resembles the common apple, and in this form it appears in Snow White and the Seven Dwarves. The princess, given an apple by the wicked witch, falls into a deep trance-like sleep which was mistaken for death. To the Ancients this soporific effect was the result of eating the mandrake, although in large doses it was believed to induce delirium. However, old Anglo-Saxon herbals endow mandrake with protective powers against demoniacal possession; in the Herbarium of Apuleius, the author recommends taking three pennies' worth in weight of mandrake in warm water as a tonic against "witlessness" or "devil sickness." In medieval times, it was considered unwise to pluck the root of the mandrake from the ground because it would let out a terrifying scream, which would strike all around stone dead. A solution was devised: an aspiring witch would

attach the mandrake to a dog's leash, then he or she would plug their ears with wax and tempt the poor animal with a succulent morsel. The dog would come bounding toward the treat and thereby free the mandrake from the earth. Of course, the dog would expire immediately from the pitiful wails of the plant, but the magician would have the prize. This practice seems only to apply to human sorcerers, as Isis and her godly compatriots were obviously immune from any ill effects.

A Spell to End Feuding

Mighty Sekhmet, desert flame, let not your hunger
    rouse you, let not your roar be heard.
Let your malice sleep, let peace and plenty reign.
Your anger once was justified, but let not your fury govern life.
Let mercy temper thy might.
Anger sleep, peace restore, harmony return to gods and men.

By his words and his will Ra expunged a portion of Sekhmet's terrible strength and, just as she had been made from his eye, great Ra created another goddess, one of stealth and cunning. This was Bast, my aunt (just as Sekhmet is my aunt) the sinuous cat-goddess of seduction and lust. In some mysterious way too this process of god creation made another deity, the lovely cow-eyed Hathor daughter of Ra. The very one who was to wed my son Horus in days to come.

And thus, almost is this story done for when Sekhmet painfully awoke, her head aching mightily she found that her anger, her lust for vengeance and her blood lust had departed.

At this juncture, I will reveal a cure for mortal beer-drinking and its ill-effects. Now this spell is a little incantation to my future daughter-in-law, beautiful Hathor. She is goddess of love and drunkenness; her dominion is the time after sunset, when Ra's boat dips below the horizon, for this is when the call of beer is most compelling. This spell is to be said during drinking-time. Do not say it the next dawn in a stupor of self-pity, for it will not work.

This is what became of my sister-goddess Sekhmet. She chose to dwell in Memphis, the city of the great architect Ptah, and soon came to the amorous attention of that god. He wed her, granting her the apt title of Lady of the Blood-stained Robe.

As for grandfather Ra, he had tired of his old age and the ways of mortals and resolved to return to eternity. The throne of the Two Lands of Upper and Lower Egypt then fell to my husband, beloved Osiris, who ruled well and was welcomed by all. Soon the world had forgotten the terrible end of the days of Ra, and all spoke of the happy things that occurred in the time of Osiris the Good.

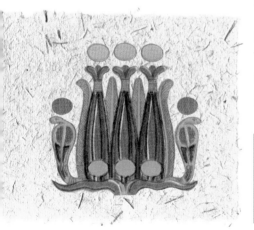

SPELL FOR DRINKING BEER

O HAIL GREAT HATHOR, Lady of Hetepet!
When Set, in the name of beer, sought to confuse a heart
Or conquer the heart of an enemy, a friend, or a ghost
He was never to be restrained.

SUCH ARE THE WORDS OF ISIS.

3 How I Became Queen of Magic and of All Egypt

In which it is told of the glory of the time of Osiris, and corpses and coffins, of betrayal and murder, and fear and flight. And how I achieved my true destiny through loss of my beloved, the magic taught to me by my guardian great Thoth, and of my wanderings.

DESTINY AND DECEPTION

If Osiris was created for me, or I for him, I cannot tell. Of the five of us our mother, Nut of the Sky, gave birth to me fourth before my sister Nephyths, and my brother Osiris was first-born.

There was little between us.

I LOVED HIM LIKE A BROTHER but he was my brother. I had passion for him as a mortal wife for her husband, but he was my husband. Of the stars that glimmered over the great Nile delta of the Lower Lands, none outshone our love.

Some have called me the goddess of love, because of the torment I endured through my loyalty to Osiris after his body left me. But in truth this mantle was only given to redeem me, and was employed only by those who believed I needed forgiveness for my subsequent actions.

Which was, to steal my grandfather Ra's secret name when his power was so weak that the light of his soul was almost extinguished. In becoming mortal he had tired of the bitter battles, the blood and the destruction of gods and humanity; and I took his sole power of creation through lies. I did this only to reanimate my beloved but if I am true here to myself, I know I became Queen of Magic for other reasons, of which you will learn later.

But judge me not harshly yet.

I will begin at the time when I fell in love. As I have told, it was when great father Ra made us mortal to live on earth that Osiris and my brothers and sisters took our khat, our physical bodies. At that moment when I gazed on Osiris, I knew his true beauty, and he mine. Now that Ra had departed the earth and returned to his Sun Boat of Million Years and was no longer earthly king, Osiris ruled as pharaoh in his place and I as queen of the Two Lands. With our brother Set and sister Nephthys, we were together and content. The people worshipped my husband because they knew the prophecy of the water-carrier at our temple at Heliopolis, our home. At Osiris' birth, she had cried out that he would be king and savior to the people of Egypt.

In devotion to my beloved Osiris, the people blessed him as great Ra. Here is a little of their incantation, which I reproduce here in my own words, for it is lengthy in its entirety.

Praise to Osiris

Hail, FOREMOST of the Westerners,
    Wennefer,
Lord of the Sacred Land!
You have appeared glorious, like Ra
He sees you and rejoices in your beauty.

The sun-disc of Ra is your sun-disc;
The rays of Ra are your rays;
The crown of Ra is your crown;
His greatness is your greatness;
His beauty is your beauty;
His throne is your throne;
His destiny is your destiny;

His West is your West;
His wisdom is your wisdom;
He will not die and you will not die.
He will triumph over his enemies
And you will triumph over your enemies;
No evil will come into being against him,
And nothing evil will come into being
    against you
Forever and ever.

THE EPIC OF ISIS AND OSIRIS

The source for the epic tale of Isis and Osiris comes in the form of an educational treatise penned by the Roman historian Mestrius Plutarch (c. 45–125 AD) at Delphi. Plutarch was a convert to Isis-worship, and in this work he details much about Egyptian culture and its systems of belief. His commitment to his scholastic research is evident in his opening address to another convert, a lady named Klea. He begins:

"Anyone who possesses intelligence, my dear Klea,
of necessity seeks all good things from the gods
but especially do we pray [for] a knowledge of the gods themselves
in so far as that is possible for human beings;
since there is nothing greater for man to receive
or more precious for a god to bestow than truth."

Osiris ruled wisely and in return he received the love of many. In his courage and diplomacy he healed the blood-lust that had taken root in the time of Ra, banishing the barbarism and fear of famine that had raged. He taught the people how to cultivate the soil, to care for their beasts, to treat the earth with tenderness and in turn worship the fruitfulness of nature. I have to admit that it was I who discovered barley and wild wheat; and as Osiris told how every plant could be sown, cultivated, and reaped, the land grew more prosperous. As the law of Maat ruled once more, it seemed as if the dark chaos caused by my infirm grandfather was over.

My spell here is for mortals, to help dispel the anger of a god. It is close to my heart, for my mother suffered so from the cursed rage of great-Ra; as have all my strange family. I suspect the people used it in the dark days of Ra's fearful fury; but I keep it safe here, inscribed in my own words, in case you should have need of it.

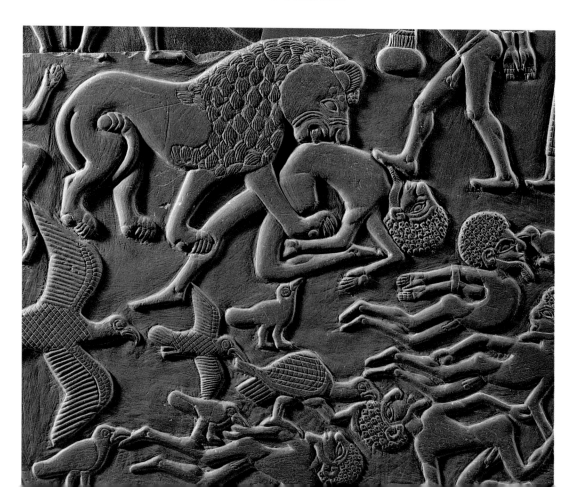

A Spell to Banish the Anger of a God

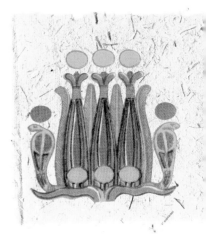

WOE TO YOU, powerful keeper of all mysteries;
A god who is angry with me has spoken a word against me.
But wrongdoing is washed away
and is now in the hands of truthful Maat.
See how I am brought to you.
Be gracious to me
And dispel all anger that is in your heart against me.

After some time, Osiris left the Two Lands. He was forever a seeker of the new, and I in my devotion could not come between him and his worldly desire. I never doubted he would return; and that once reunited, with the blessing of the Khonsu, great deity of the moon, we would have the child Horus I yearned for. I had my family around me, and little thought my brother Set harbored us ill-will and envy for the throne. His obsession was kept secret, knowing that quiet slander would be his best weapon. Why had Osiris deserted Heliopolis for so long, when a ruler who was surely his equal could be found? Now that ruler was not I, although I preserved the land and ruled as a Queen. That usurper was my own brother, and brother of my husband. And as he pursued his campaign of hatred, I must confess that I did not suspect his motives.

My sister Nephthys was equally innocent, yet it was her dissatisfaction that sparked the tragedy of Osiris's death. This is how it came about: Set, in his eagerness to find favor against my husband, consorted with Queen Aso of Ethiopia. As his audiences with her became more frequent, my neglected sister – also wanting her rightful child – lay with my husband on his return.

Osiris' homecoming was celebrated throughout Egypt. It was the twenty-eighth year of his reign, and the people had not forgotten him. The celebrations lasted throughout the many journeys of Ra through the firmament, and this was opportunity enough for Set and Nephthys to ply him with intoxicants.

BOTH HAD THEIR SINISTER AND SEPARATE REASONS, AS I WAS TO DISCOVER.

My sister, on seeing Osiris retire to his chamber, adorned herself in my garments and anointed her body with my perfumed oils. She then entered Osiris' chamber and lay with him, praying for the help of the deity of fertility. "Please give me this child, oh goddess," she implored, "for Osiris is my only hope of motherhood." Little did she know that her husband Set was hiding there, stung by her words and intent on malice and murder. When Nephthys departed, Set's jealousy knew no bounds. As my beloved rested, he measured every part of his body as he cursed him.

He took his measurements to a coffin-maker, and instructed him to make up the finest door to the afterlife that any mortal could know. It was inlaid with precious stones and painted in vibrant detail, so much so that others coveted it as a work of art; although in truth it was intended to be my husband's final resting place. As the wife of Set grew big with the seed of Osiris, so the death-chest became ever-opulent. And by the judgment of Maat, she had no inkling that Set knew of her unborn's true parentage.

NEPHTHYS' RECIPE FOR A CHILD

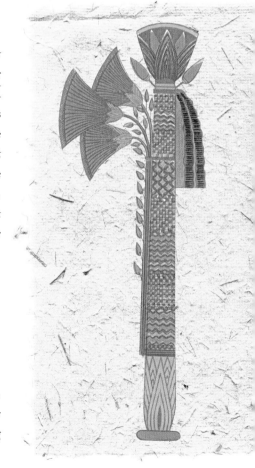

TO HAVE TAKEN MY SEMBLANCE and seduced my beloved Osiris, Nephthys would have remembered a lesson or two from my aunt Bast, goddess of cats, fertility and joy. I know this to be true, because later in my existence Bastis became known by my name, Baen Aset, which means "the soul of Isis." Not that I advocate my sister's deception, but this small ceremony may be practiced by women to entice the favor of my aunt so they may have the man of their choosing. The following may be collected and placed by an image of aunt Bast, great deity whose khat is the body of a woman and her head that of a sacred cat.

SWEET-SMELLING OILS and perfumes, to be placed in a bas-jar (a stoppered bottle named after Bast)
A taste of honey
Mint, for cats do like it

Then powerful words are said, of the woman's own making. She tells of the man she desires, and asks Bastis for her guidance and blessing. She may light a candle before uttering her incantation, and extinguish it when she is done.

The Corpse
— and the —
Coffer

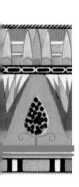

THIS PART OF MY TALE I TELL WITH DEEP REGRET. HAD I HEEDED MY INSTINCT ABOUT MY DARK BROTHER SET, AND LOOKED TO THE OBVIOUS, MAYBE IT COULD HAVE BEEN DIFFERENT. SO THE SPELL FOR IMMORTALITY THAT FOLLOWS THESE WORDS IS BOTH A WISH AND A WARNING.

I WILL PROCEED.

THE CHILD ANUBIS was born to Nephthys, beautiful in his innocence, and a great feast was held by Set in the city of Avaris to celebrate his coming. Set invited his wily cohorts, those whom he had coerced into distrusting Osiris in his absence. Yet as the feast began, I hoped that the birth of Anubis had assuaged Set's dark ambition; so I brushed my aside my doubt.

As the company enjoyed the food and drink, my brother set about instigating a game. "This exquisite coffer has been given here as a gift by Ethiopia's matchless queen," he began, nodding to Queen Aso who returned his ingratiating smile. "Whosoever fits it shall gain it as a prize." And then the challengers presented themselves – tall and thin like the reeds of the delta, wide of girth, all with great merriment.

58

None, of course, did fit the coffer.

Then wily Set left his seat at the table and approached his brother Osiris. "Oh great King," he announced, his formality a point of great amusement to the assembled guests. "Being perfect in character in every way, should not the fit of the coffer be perfect? Step within and prove to the company of Heliopolis and the city of Avaris that this great artifact is indeed worthy of your matchless spirit." Set's eloquence was a dart through my heart. In speed I turned to Osiris and implored him with my eyes, as speak I could not. My feeling of foreboding was more keen than the shape-shifting of Ra's eye into the once-demonic Sekhmet, my sister-goddess of destruction. But my beloved husband, ever the inquisitive, stood up proudly to meet his challenge with one hundred eyes upon him.

Laughing, he regarded the coffer and placed one foot within, then lay down along its full length. It fitted his body in every dimension, as if ready-made; which of course it was. And Set's pleasure, his long-awaiting vengeance, rasped from his throat as an asp makes ready for the kill. "This coffer is surely made for you, and you it," he began, " so it is only right that it becomes your eternal home." His face reddened with anger as he hurled the lid of the coffer down upon poor Osiris as his co-conspirators surrounded it so none dared to challenge his cruelty. As molten lead was poured over the box to seal it, so Osiris' fate was sealed. I heard screams as I fled the palace without knowing they were my own.

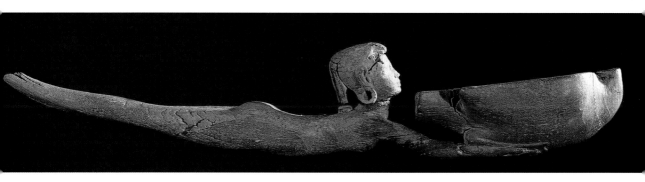

THE PLEA OF ISIS

In Adolf Erman's Ancient Egyptian Poetry and Prose is this plea from Isis, spoken when Osiris was trapped in Set's coffer and so put to death. It is likely that this is a Greek interpretation of the story. The term "pillar" refers to a point later in the story, when the body of Osiris in the coffer is adopted by a tree, which is cut down to form a central pillar in the palace of the King of Byblos. Osiris is also represented as a pillar in the Djed amulet (see page 152). Isis' entreaty for Osiris to come to his house is thought to refer to his rightful place as king of the Two Lands and to their mortal relationship and husband and wife.

COME TO YOUR HOUSE

Come to your house,
Come to your house,
O Pillar!

Come to your house,
beautiful bull,

Lord of mankind,
beloved lord of women!

Come to your house,
Come to your house,
O Pillar!

Some mortals worshipped me for the tears I shed. Days and nights I wept as Ra in his sunboat journeyed through light and darkness. With the water from my eyes I watered the great plains of the Two Lands and the soil became rich and food plentiful. Mortals had then everything for their sustenance, yet I had nothing. Later, they called me the deity of fertility and creation.

I wanted Osiris to live again as a man and would not rest until I found his coffer. As Set took my husband's place on the throne of the Two Lands, I began my wanderings. Season after season, I asked every mortal if they had seen the coffer. I must have looked like a beggar, a madwoman with torn and bloodied garments ranting about a box that I had as much chance of finding as my own sanity. My sister Nephthys and her infant son Anubis too suffered as Set disowned both of them. I pass quickly from this part of the story as it brings me only pain in its recollection.

I found Osiris' coffer. Set had cast it into the Nile, and from there it was carried north through the delta into Lower Egypt into the Great Green Sea of Asia. It came to rest in remote Byblos, where a tamarisk bush held it and its great essence. The tamarisk florished with the godly treasure within, and grew tall and beautiful, like my beloved Osiris. A carpenter was instructed to cut the trunk intact and take it to the court of the King, where it was to be a central pillar in his palace.

ISIS AS MADONNA

Isis shares many attributes with the Virgin Mary. Isis may have been the forerunner of Mary, or the two icons may have merged to embody similar virtues and to entwine differing cultures. In art, Mary is depicted holding Jesus, just as figurines of Isis portray her with the infant Horus on her lap. Mary and Isis' robes are also blue, and they share the title stella maris, or star of the sea. Mary, mother of Jesus is associated with the moon, as is Isis, who was born when Thoth stole five extra days of the year from the moon-god Khonsu in an enchanted dice game (see pages 20–24). And as Mother Mary was a virgin, miraculously giving birth to a child, so Isis became magically pregnant by her dead husband, Osiris. Mary and Isis are protectors of women and children, and preside over motherhood.

Mary Magdalen, however, has the love goddess Hathor as her Egyptian twin. Her planet is sultry Venus and traditionally she is shown wearing red, which is Hathor's color. The term "scarlet woman" may have come from an amalgam of these two classical seductresses.

Children playing on the banks of the Nile had told me of the coffer's progress, which is why I walked to Byblos, and again it was to be a child who led me to rightfully take Osiris back to Egypt. It happened like this: the women of the court saw me weeping and took pity on me, giving me food and water, and in return I dressed their hair and listened to their worries. Soon the queen of Byblos asked to see me, and I told her my story. To my delight, she took me in as nursemaid to her beautiful son whom I loved with all my heart.

Now I always repay my debts. To the children who had directed me to Osiris' floating coffer, I gave the gift of prophecy. To the queen's baby son, the least I could do was make him immortal. I built a fire in the great hall and transformed my shape into a swallow, the better to fan the flames with my wings. I took up the infant to place him into the flames, but the queen had discovered my little ritual and screaming rushed to her son's aid. Then I had no choice but to reveal my true identity as Isis. "Do you not know who I am? Mistress of magic and divine queen of all Egypt, beloved of Osiris?" The queen trembled as she clung to her son in shock at what she had witnessed, which was just as well because then she had to ask for my forgiveness. My prize was Osiris' exquisite chest, which was cut from the central pillar of the great palace.

This is my spell for immortality. If the Queen had not disturbed me her son would now be blessed with eternal life, borne from my love for him and my gratitude to her. It is chanted after the death of the *khat,* the physical body, and is such a funerary rite to the afterlife at which Anubis my nephew presides.

SPELL FOR IMMORTALITY

I HAVE COME TO BE your divine
protector
I waft unto you the air of life
And the north wind which comes forth from
the god Tem to your nose.
I have made whole for you your windpipe
and I make you live like a god.
Your enemies have fallen under your feet.
I have made your word to be true
before Nut
And you are mighty before the gods.

With Osiris, I traveled by royal barque back to Helipolis, leaving behind the remnants of the great pillar at Byblos. The king and queen paid me due honor by erecting a temple there in my name, which housed the precious wood that had so protected my beloved.

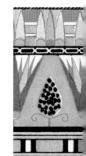

Now it was time to execute the final part of my plan: to bring Osiris back to life. This reanimation was new to me, but I believed by the power of mighty Ra that it could be done. I had seen the workings of great magic in the name of my uncle Thoth and of that creator-god Khnum, who with his own potter's wheel fashioned humanity from clay and with his breath gave them life.

In my old chamber at the palace was the phial of spittle collected from my great father Ra when I nursed him in his mortal sickness. I had mixed his spittle with a little clay, and kept it tight in a box. Hiding the coffer of Osiris in a thicket outside the palace grounds, I stole into my room and retrieved the box from its hiding place. I ran with it under my arm until my breath was almost gone.

As mighty Ra's power weakening with the dimming of the sun, I vowed to take his power. Although no longer mortal, I knew he would soon present himself on earth again. With this is mind, I took the precious clay and from it fashioned an asp, its pointed head vicious like an arrow. I named it and gave it life, just as all creation had been made. To my amazement and relief, the asp uncoiled and darted over the cool desert plain. I took it in my palm and walked to the crossroads, where I set down my asp and hid in readiness for the appearance of Ra.

In due course the dim form of the sun-god came visible, sinking weakly toward the horizon and stepping tentatively on the earth. At the crossroads, the asp did my bidding and sank its poisonous fangs into the ankle of Ra. I watched from a thicket as Ra's body spasmed in agony; he then called out the names of the gods to help him.

His voice trembled as the gods assembled, and all the time he cried out, " but I did not see the serpent that assailed me," and "by the waters of Nun, this evil was not created by my own hand." He knew the bite of the asp was deadly, and that it could cause him eternal suffering. The poison flooded Ra's body, inflaming his limbs and parching his mouth. The master of all creation was close to mortal death, as I had wished. He implored that I be called upon to save him.

And so I came with my amulets and magical words of power, feigning no knowledge of the cause of his condition. Ra told me how the asp had crossed his path. " I am bathed in the sweat of summer, though I am cold; was the snake of fire, or water? My eye fails and I cannot see the sky." As Ra passed into his delirium, I said to him, "Let me cast out this poison. Tell me your true name, so this evil will be delivered by your own greatness." Then he told me all his names under the sun. The maker of heaven and earth, and everything that walks upon it; creator of the hours and days; Kephera the scarab at morning, Ra at noontide and Atum at dusk. And so on. But this was not the information that I was looking for, and Ra knew it.

I CAME TO THE POINT.

His light was so dim, I could look at him directly, into those spheres that once were almighty. "What you have told me is not your real name," I implored. "O tell it to me now, so that I may save your eternal light." The poison was seeping deeper into the very heart of Ra, and all the while his bony fingers shook like clamoring keys. He writhed and railed in the dust; his feeble rays darkened to strange speckles in the twilight and I, a cold observer of his agony, his descendant, stood by.

He would surrender to me, against all his will. I said this inside my mind over and over like a prayer.

"FROM MY LIPS, MY TRUE NAME WILL PASS. OH ISIS, I WILL ENTRUST IT TO YOU," HE CROAKED, "AS WITHOUT YOUR ENCHANTMENT I WILL NEVER RISE AGAIN."

AND HE OBEYED.

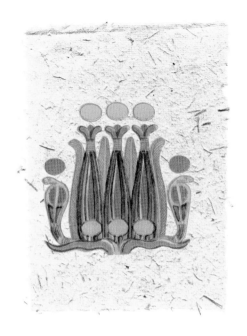

"Then tell me now, oh great father." Now I spoke this calmly as if it were no great matter, but I shook inside; the prize was so golden, yet Ra so stubborn, in my heart I could not truly conceive the weight of his words. I was to hold the power of all creation that no other god, save mighty Ra, would have. I then reached to take his arm so we could set ourselves apart from the company of gods, just as I had nursed him during his mortal sickness. He dragged his body like a creeping bundle of glimmering rags toward a shelter of papyrus plants, his form diminishing as Thoth himself measured the final minutes of his life.

We were all alone, eerie in the half-light. And this was my moment; it would never return. I had to have all that I desired for the power of Ra would protect me and mine. I too would shine, a goddess with light possessed. Never again would I be beholden to wrathful Ra, borrowing his favor day by day. I remembered my mother Nut, banished to the air, and my father Geb, trodden into the earth, and vowed to take the secret name of my jealous great father. I breathed softy to still my heart, and put forward my final request.

"Oh Ra, in return for my healing I ask that my unborn son, Horus, is given the power of your eyes. So he shall have the sun for his left eye, and for the right, the moon," I breathed. "It is but little, is it not?"

WEARILY HE NODDED IN ASSENT.

He was about to endow me with the greatest power of the universe, so this small favor was a sundry gift. I admit it was an afterthought on my part, which I was soon glad of, as you will see.

I bent close to Ra then, and set my ear by his parched lips. I could barely see him, and had to touch his dull crown with my fingertips to trace his outline.

As blackness descended, he spoke to me one vital word: his true name.

I felt as if a bolt of lightning had eclipsed me, I wanted to run and fly to Osiris, to be full of this new magic. But cure Ra I must for without him, nothing was possible. The great Boat of a Million Years must ride the firmament and give out its divine sunlight.

So there by the whispering papyri I chanted my spell of healing. I watched Ra at every pause in my incantation, and the poison drained slowly from his body. As his pain eased the flush of life pinked his skin, and his spark of existence crept back into his fragile form. In mere moments, the generative force of the universe was returned.

My work done, I fled the presence of Ra. And with the knowledge of Ra's secret name, truly had I gained power over all creation. I would reanimate my beloved Osiris; but more of this later. I cannot reveal here the true name of Ra, as it is also the root of my goddess-power and my status as queen of magic.

But next to please you I will tell of a spell against snake bites, in which figures of clay are made in the likeness of myself, great Isis, my great father Ra, and Horus, my unborn son.

From Ra to Amen

In the Old Kingdom capital of Heliopolis, Ra was known as Atum-Ra. This describes Ra in his aspect as creator-god, emerging from the watery chaos of Nun in the center of a lotus flower. The prefix Atum is also Ra's local name, and over successive dynasties this changed to reflect newly emergent cities and rulers. During the New Kingdom and the rise of Thebes as the metropolis of the south under the rule of pharaoh Mentuhotep II (2055–2004 BCE), he became associated with the Theban god Amun, and so inherited the new title of Amun-Ra. By 1965 BCE, Amun-Ra was described as the "king of the gods." An alternative spelling of Amun (or Zeus-Ammon, as he was known in the Ptolemaic dynasty) is Amen. Sigmund Freud has suggested that the "Amen" recited at the end of prayers was originally a reference to Ra. So today, we may still be celebrating the divine will of Ra every time we pray.

4 THE SPELLS OF PROTECTION AGAINST ALL POISONS

IN WHICH IT IS TOLD OF SET AND
SORCERY, OF SNAKES AND SCORPIONS,
OF MALICE AND HEALING MAGIC.
IT IS TOLD OF HOPE AND
HARDSHIP, OF TERROR
AND TRANSFORMATIONS AND OF
THE GREATEST OF ALL MAGICS,
(THRICE TOLD)
THE MAKING TO LIVE AGAIN.

SET
AND THE
VENOM
OF THE
SNAKE

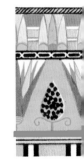

THE ILLS OF THE WORLD MAY INFLICT VILE HARM; SO, IN
MEASURE, ARE THERE SPELLS OF GREAT HEALING. THOSE
INSCRIBED WITHIN ARE TO REPEL ATTACK FROM BEASTS, INSECTS,
AND CREEPING REPTILES IN PARTICULAR, IN WHICH CATEGORY I
ALSO INCLUDE MY MALICIOUS BROTHER SET. HIS DEMONIC PLOT
TO MURDER MY BELOVED OSIRIS TAUGHT ME HOW THE VENOM OF
THE SNAKE STRIKES IN HUMAN GUISE.

YET PROTECTION MUST ALWAYS BE THE MASTER OF CURE. BEFORE
I CONTINUE MY DIVINE ODYSSEY, LET ME TELL YOU OF THIS LITTLE
RITUAL THAT WILL SEEK OUT MALICE BEFORE ITS FRUIT DELIVERS
THE BITTEREST POISON.

A Spell to Make the Guilty Confess

THIS CUNNING TRICK is easy to master but may easily go awry if the bearer of the spell-amulet uses poisonous ink, or any matter that induces illness or death in its making. It is excellent for making a mortal confess to all manner of secrets and lies.

WHAT HAPPENS IS THIS. The person who doubts must inscribe on papyrus their question. The papyrus is then folded small, and placed in a jug of water. The water is poured from the jug into a drinking vessel, and he or she presents it to the object of the spell to be drunk as ordinary water. If the person is guilty, they will have no choice but to confess their misdoings before you.

DO NOT USE THIS SPELL IF YOU ARE UNPREPARED TO RISK A PAINFUL TRUTH.

JUST AS I USED THE GREATEST MAGIC to drive out the serpent-venom from great Ra, as I have told, I would truly use it to save the life of any god or mortal. Many have since worshipped my snake-cure (although I again confess that it was truly trickery, as the asp was of my own making).

Those devoted to me may have practiced this ritual I think, by the fashioning of clay idols and the playing out of a small dumb-show. The incantation that goes with it is intoned, although naturally without the true secret name of Ra. This divine driving out of the serpent venom became the very symbol of my sorcery, in the form of a sharp-headed and straight serpent that I carry with me always. Mortals may hold me dear by creating my image, which pleases me greatly; which is why I write it here.

A Spell Against Snake Bites

From clay, the figure of great Isis is made.
From clay, the figure of Horus, my son-to-be, is made.
From clay, the figure of Temu-Ra, the evening sun, is made.
From clay, the figure of Horus the Elder, steersman in the
    boat of Ra, is made.

Over these figures, was spoken this incantation:

In the name of great Isis, may this poison depart from Ra
Oh Eye of Horus, go hence from the god, and shine outside
    his mouth
It is Isis who makes fall the poison upon the earth.
Ra lives, and the poison dies
The poison dies, and Ra lives!

These are the words of Isis, the mistress of the gods, who knew Ra by his own name.

SNAKES, CROCODILES, AND THE AFTERLIFE

In the Egyptian Book of the Dead are a number of spells intended to protect the deceased as they passed into the underworld, the realm of Osiris. In addition to the many incantations used to protect the heart, body, and soul of the dead, there are also specific spells that repel snakes and other predators. In the afterlife, it was thought that the dead person continued to live his former life – should he be judged worthy by Osiris – and therefore the assailants that had plagued the living were also thought to continue to plague the dead. There are spells to drive away crocodiles, rerek-snakes, songstress snakes, a cobra, and a beetle. Some spells are simply dismissive and mildly insulting, such as Spell 33, in which the deceased claims that the rerek-snake has eaten a mouse and chewed the bones of a putrefying cat. In the more serious case of a crocodile coming to steal magic, the incantation is more vehement. The gods are invoked for the four principle directions of the compass:

"Get back, crocodile of the West ... My detestation of you is within my belly, for I have the power of Osiris, and I am Set."

It is likely that in calling upon these two brother-gods that the deceased would summon the protective power of Osiris and the destructive forces of Set in order to deter the crocodile.

Back to my story, for by the word of great thoth, master of scribes, must it be told.

It was time at last to use my new-found power of creation to reanimate Osiris. After seasons of wandering to find his poor body, I now had him back; he was almost home to me, save for the spell that I was now so desperate to recite. I had left him lifeless and alone while tricking great Ra to speak his name, and now I saw him in my mind, his pure spirit returned. Yet when I reached the hiding place of his coffer, there to perform my magic, I found not his body but my weeping sister Nephthys.

"Oh Isis", she began. "He has come again and Osiris is no more." I looked at her in disbelief.

"How could your vile husband have come here?" I screamed. "I have the name of Ra and Osiris will live!" Grasping the dry leaves of the thicket-bushes, I crawled within the void where the precious coffer had lain. I cried to the gods, and wailed and clawed the earth that should have kept him safe. Even the touch of the stony earth, the realm of my father Geb, tortured me and blood coursed from my fingers and palms. In my madness, my bleeding was a sanguine reminder of Set. He had left his mark on me.

Nephthys stroked my head and made me quiet. She told me her story.

Set had come across the coffer while hunting and in a bloody rage had torn the body of Osiris into fourteen pieces, scattering the sundered body over the lands of Egypt.

Nephthys sobbed as she told me of his malice; how he had seemed animal, not god, in his rage of destruction.

We sat motionless, looking at the meandering Nile. Now, again, I have nothing, I thought. Even the sky closed in as mighty Ra hid in shame behind deceitful clouds.

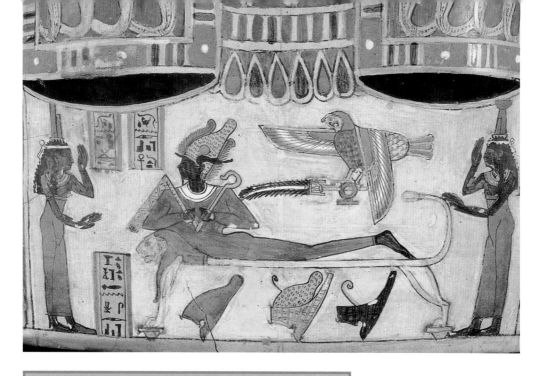

WOULD OSIRIS EVER HAVE IMMORTAL REST?

So my second wanderings began. But this time I felt the fire of anger against Set, and the tears I had wept over the Nile plains were of the past. Fuelled by fury and with dark Nephthys and jackal-headed Anubis, her son, beside me, we three began an odyssey to collect together the body of Osiris. In a reed boat we sailed the Nile, and all the animals heard our cries and helped us search. Wherever we found a part of Osiris, a beautiful temple was built and each time I performed the burial rites for every fragment of his divine khat. This is one of the reasons that I am known as the great mistress of the underworld, called Ament, or hidden goddess. I became famous thereafter for helping the transformation of the dead to make ready for the afterlife, the realm of my beloved Osiris. Here is one of the funeral texts for protection that is used on such occasions and I repeat it here, and you will see the reason when you have read it.

THE SPEECH OF THE FLAME

I COME TO hew in pieces.
I have not been hewn in pieces
And I will not permit thee to be hewn in pieces.
I come to do violence to your enemies
Yet I will not permit violence to be done unto you.
I protect you.

MUMMIFICATION

Mummification comprised an intricate series of rituals performed by embalmers and a company of priests. It was a costly process, taking some seventy days to complete, and was therefore the province of wealthy nobles and pharaohs.

Firstly, the vital organs would be removed from the body and preserved in four special canopic jars, which would accompany the mummified form on its journey to the afterlife. The heads of the Four Sons of Horus – human-headed Imsety, jackal-headed Duamutef, baboon-headed Hapy, and hawk-headed Qebehsenuef – adorned each one to symbolize their protection of the liver, stomach, lungs, and intestines respectively. The heart was left intact, as this was seen as the seat of the emotions and intelligence, and on it was placed the emblem of the scarab during the final funerary rituals. The brain, however, was not prized and was removed in a delicate operation through the nose, then discarded.

Natron, a special dehydrating salt, when then applied to the corpse; this substance occurred naturally in the Nile and consisted of four salts that absorbed the remaining fluids in the body and prevented putrefaction. When the deceased was completely dry and shrunken, the body was stuffed with resin, sawdust and linen, and shaped into its original form. At this stage, false eyes may have been added.

Each part of the person, including the head, was then mummified in linen layers. Within the layers special amulets for protection were placed and prayers intoned by attending priests. When the process was complete, the body was enveloped in a shroud.

The best-preserved examples are from the eighteenth to the twentieth dynasties of the New Kingdom (c 1570–1075 BCE), including those of Tuthankhamun and other pharaohs of the era.

It is rumored that the head of Osiris lays at Abydos, and his right leg rests on the island of Elephantine, as all in the Two Lands wanted claim to a part of him. But Nephthys, Anubis and I took with us every limb, every fragment of the great god and enjoined the parts one by one. Anubis, skilled at the arts of embalmment and mummification, was charged with this responsibility. It is how he became known as the god of burial rituals across all Egypt.

I found my entire husband; or nearly, excepting his phallus, which had been swallowed by the mouth of a great fish. By my words of power, I named what I wanted and thus it was created, so Osiris was whole again. I took to the sky as a bird, beating my wings to give him breath and sending him the light of existence from my feathered sheen. Through this sacred magic, I raised the dead and made him live again. That night our embrace brought us our child Horus; and at last had I my beloved child inside me.

Mortals have since copied my magic, although of course without the secret name of Ra. Queen Hapshepsut wisely followed my example in her mortuary temple, which houses a temple dedicated to lovely Hathor, one of the more pleasing members of my family. There the local women bring offerings of phalluses they have constructed themselves from wood. Their endeavors are often rewarded, I am told, with the reanimation of love and the bringing of children into the world.

Yet for Osiris, his physical body was not truly complete; the father of my unborn child was not to remain on earth as a living mortal. As Ra's Sun Boat of a Million Years traversed the sky, so Osiris was spirited to the underworld. Here he became gatekeeper to the afterlife, and god of resurrection. Osiris was to live for evermore in peace; and so, in turn, I could now rest for a short while.

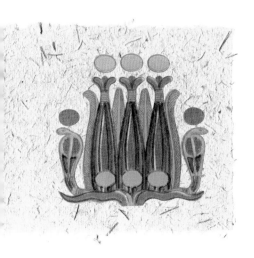

THAT WAS, UNTIL KING SET CAME BACK INTO MY LIFE.

My sister Nephthys, her son Anubis and I then lived as outcasts, living from the fertile soils of the Nile plains for that season. The sadness of Osiris' final parting was mingled with our shared sense of content. My father Geb, great deity of the earth, protected us. Our bellies were full and our souls blissful, for Osiris lived on.

THE SEVEN HALLS OF OSIRIS

Osiris ruled the realm of the afterlife. In one part of his kingdom, also referred to as the Seventh Pylon, or seventh hour of the night, were seven halls through which the dead must pass to continue their journey. Each was guarded by a doorkeeper, a watcher, and a herald. The deceased had to satisfy each one before he could move onto the next. Offerings including the thigh, head, heart, and hoof of a red bull were made at each hall, with incantations. Yet the key to each hall was a spoken mantra which was the names of the seven doorkeepers, seven watchers, and seven heralds.

Gods of the first hall: Sekhet-hra-asht-aru, meaning "he whose face is many shaped"; the eavesdropper, Semetu, and loud-voiced Hu-kheru.

Gods of the second hall: Tun-hat, which translates as "he whose hind parts are extended"; Seqet-hra, meaning "shifting of face"; and Sabes, meaning "burner."

Gods of the third hall: Am-huat-ent-pehfi, or "he who eats the corruption of his hinder-parts"; vigilant Res-hra, and cursing Uaau.

Gods of the fourth hall: Khesef-hra-saht-kheru, who protects a person from noise; Res-ab the wakeful, and grim Neteka-hra-khesef-atu, who rebukes attackers.

Gods of the fifth hall: Ank-em-fentu, the snake-eater; Ashebu, the fiery; and Hippopotamus-faced Tebherkehaat, whose name means "raging of power."

Gods of the sixth hall: Akentauk-ha-kheru, "the bread-shaper, the harsh-voiced"; the lookout An-hra, and sharp-eyed Metes-hra-ari-she, protector of the lake.

Gods of the seventh hall: Metes-sen, or "he who cuts them down"; loud-voiced Aaaa-kheru, and Khesef-hra-khemiu, the defender.

Ra rode his sun boat high at noontimes during that fateful Summer, his mighty power sprouting lush stalks of delta reed, wheat, barley, berries and other such gifts of the land. Each day, as my unborn child Horus grew within me, we three would wander to the papyrus copse to shelter from the searing rays of Ra. We talked of the future, of our hopes for Horus and the destiny that awaited him as king of the Two Lands.

Set discovered our afternoon idylls and spoke shameful words, which I shall not repeat, as in so doing his memory is ever more disgraced. As King of the Two Lands he had civil power over us and, in short, imprisoned Nephthys and I as flax-spinners so that we may earn our daily bread in captivity. Now I was seething with anger but would not reveal it to wily Set; after all, my child kicked within my belly and, as great Ra had promised me, one day Horus would overthrow Set, ending his tyrannical rule. I endured the grind of each day and the turning of great Khonsu, master of the moon, until in due course my baby was born to me in captivity. As great Ra decreed, he was named Horus.

As I was spinning one day, with little Horus sleeping at my feet, a ghost of a shadow crept upon me. Thoth the Wise materialized in my poor dwelling, and his voice swept into the void.

"O Isis, as I, great scribe and measurer of time, gave you birth, I come before you to give you warning," he proclaimed gravely. (You may recall how uncle Thoth used his cunning in a dice-game to steal five days so my mother could deliver me without breaking the curse of Ra. I took heed, as timing was surely his strong point.)

"It is time for you to leave this house, for Set intends to corrupt this child. Your penance is over, and now Horus must thrive."

I NEEDED NO FURTHER PROMPTING.

Leaving the spinning wheel turning and all our victuals, with Horus in my arms I fled. I know that the words that Thoth had spoken were a potent spell of protection; yet for how long? I kept running in silence and dread.

MALICE
— AND THE —
SEVEN SCORPIONS

THIS INCANTATION OF THOTH GUARDED ME AGAINST THE VENOM OF ENVY WHEN I AND MY BELOVED CHILD HORUS FLED THE FURY OF THE DARK SET, AND TOOK TO THE DELTA SWAMP. I GIVE IT MY FULL ATTENTION HERE.

YOU WHO ARE READING may remember that this fragment of my story began with my escape from the house of flax-weaving, when Thoth warned me of Set's evil intent to corrupt my child. Horus and I must have presented a deadly aspect; we had wandered for what seemed an eternity, hiding during the heat of the day and making our way through the dank earth and rushes by the light of the moon god. It is to him, great Thoth, that I express my gratitude, for he taught me this spell. He bestows his luminous presence on whoever shall use it.

PROVIDED THEY ARE DESERVING.

Now this spell of my uncle Thoth brought seven deadly female scorpions to my aid. These creatures followed my every progress, ever ready to bring death to any pursuer who had in mind harm to my child or myself. My gratitude to these scorpions is also eternal.

Each scorpion was possessed of a name, for so it has been since Ra gave life to the first creatures. These names were Mestet, Mestetef, Petet, Thetet, Matet, Befen and the terrible Tefenet. This last was most deadly of all, for she was their queen and bore the poisons of all the others upon her wicked claws.

With Horus swaddled to me, I traveled through the swamps of Crocodopolis and then to the City of the Two Sandals, on the border of the country of Athu. I did not know then that the sandals by which the metropolis was named were made of the leather flayed from the skin of my dark brother Set.

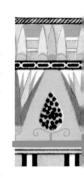

We approached a settlement for shelter and perhaps a little bread or raw grain. Petet, Thetet, and Matet guided my journey. Yet upon my asking, the chieftain's wife, named Usert the Strong, cursed me and called me an outcast, a foul witch. In her arrogance and fury she hurled sharp stones to drive me away and I was banished without food or water, and left the site in humiliation. I recount this tale from the past, yet even as I write I know again the shame inflicted by her envy and hatred.

That night, Horus and I slept in an abandoned hut set far back in the swamps. During the night – unknown to me – the scorpion-queen Tefenet boiled with rage at the way we had been treated, and resolved to avenge the insult. She stormed back to the settlement and there struck the son of Usert as he lay sleeping. Seven venoms mingled in the child's body while the very vapor of the poison was so potent that the reed hut ignited into flames.

It was indeed fortunate that even as the satisfied Tefenet returned to me, the redoubtable Usert awoke to see the peril, and dragged her son's fevered body from the fire. Only then did she see that the poor child was blue with scorpion venom. Loudly she lamented, but no man or woman came to her. Across the swamp I heard her cries, as indeed I do for all; so even in my anger I had to go to her. I told Usert that my father had taught me the secret of driving out poison (a statement that was not exactly a lie, but not quite true, either.) I placed my hands upon the body, and invoked the names of my scorpion servants.

THE SCORPION GODDESS

Selket was the scorpion-goddess of magic. She is depicted as a woman with a scorpion on her head, and sometimes as a lion.

Her name means "she who breathes," which perhaps implies her ambiguity – spitting deadly venom at her assailants, yet fiercely protecting her allies from harm or death. An image of Selket is carved upon the canopic shrine of Tutankhamun, along with that of Isis, her sister Nephthys, and Neith, goddess of war. She exists there as the goddess protector of Qebesenef, one of the Four Sons of Horus who guarded the king's internal organs in the canopic jars within the shrine (see Mummification, page 77). Inside this shrine lay four tiny gold coffins, and on each was a spell to invoke the goddess and the Son of Horus whom she protected. Selket's spell reads, "My two arms are upon what is in me. I protect Qebesenef who is inside me. Qebesenef Osiris King Neb Kheperu Re, true of voice." This last name, "Osiris King Neb Kheperu Re," is actually the true name of the deceased Tuthankhamun, the ren (see page 30) – a necessary ingredient in the magic of his survival in the afterlife.

My little cantrip worked, as I knew it would. This was the first time that I had used it, but I have since found that it is potent against more than the venom of scorpions. If an enemy slanders you or if people harken to words that lead to your infamy, this spell can be spoken to remove the sting of words and cause the poison that enters men's ears to fall away.

THE SPELL OF THE SCORPION

❶ POISON OF TEFENET come out
Come out of him and fall upon the ground.
Poison of Befen advance not, penetrate no
further.
Come out of him and fall upon the fround.
Venom of Mastet hasten not.
Venom of Mestetef rise not.
Venom of Petet and Thetet approach not.
Venom of Matet come out and fall upon
the ground.
For did I not instruct you to look not on
children of any other harmless thing?
I am Isis; mistress of magic, speaker of
spells whose voice can awake the dead.
The child shall live, the poison shall die.
As Horus is strong and well for me,
so shall the child be strong and well for his
mother.

My work with Usert and her son was done; it was time to move on. Yet, wherever I rested I could not be safe, forever wondering of my brother Set's evil intent toward me and my dear Horus.

HORUS
— AND THE —
ENEMY
SCORPION

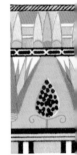

THIS I CONFESS IS NOT A TALE THAT I RELISH RE-TELLING, BUT DO
IT I MUST. IT IS OF A TIME WHEN I WAS MOST TESTED, AS MOTHER
TO HORUS AND AS QUEEN OF MAGIC. FOR MY POWERS TO AID MY
SICKENING SON WERE BUT USELESS. WISE THOTH WAS AGAIN
OUR SALVATION, AND TO HIS SPIRIT I DEDICATE THE MAGNIFICENT
SPELL SET OUT HERE. IT WAS, TOO A SIGN OF HIS UNERRING
FIDELITY TO HORUS' SWEET LIFE AND OUR JUST CAUSE. IT HOLDS
A SPECIAL PLACE IN MY MEMORY.

As outlaws from the court of Set we journeyed on, Horus and I, to Khemmis, by the Great Green Sea. When we first came upon it, it was a forlorn fastness, save its little water-pools that the birds drank from. Yet this strange backwater soon felt like home. For the first time since my son's birth, I began to feel strangely protected, which as you know is not a sentiment I often experience unless I know a spell has been cast. But I had my reward in little Horus who was fast growing into a strong lively boy. My only regret was leaving him every noontide to scour the plain for food, foraging and begging from anyone I happened to meet.

One afternoon I returned to a quiet dwelling, and immediately I was suspicious as Horus was ever vivacious. As I entered the hut, in horror I saw his little body on the ground, still as death. I screamed and screamed for help and the people of the papyrus swamps came running. None spoke a word to me for their sorrow was so heavy and in my grief I could not speak the secret name of Ra and reanimate my own son. I was lost like a mortal as all my goddess-power deserted me.

A woman of a noble family came; she said she had the knowledge to save him but in my heart I knew true dread, for if I could not rekindle the life in my son, what chance had she? All the village then shouted in disbelief, for they knew Horus and I were protected from Set, that the word of mighty sun-god Ra must surely be our shield. It was revealed that Horus had been stung by a scorpion that was unknown to me.

My sister Nephthys was called for, she too still an outcast from her wicked husband Set. Weeping and wailing through the papyrus swamps, she lamented Horus' death; and with her was my friend the great scorpion-goddess Selket. They came to me and immediately looked to devise magic by which my son would live again. Selket, of all deities, must have had knowledge of driving out the venom of the scorpion, but in the face of such dire sorcery, she too was lost. Yet soon a plan was formed, drastic in its design; but we had no other way.

WE DECIDED TO MAKE TIME STAND STILL.

A Prayer to Make Time Stand Still

Oh COME INTO THE Boat of a
   Million Years
These words of the great Isis, Selket,
   Nephthys
Let not the boat of mighty Ra continue
   its course
Let the mariners of the boat of mighty
   Ra row no more
Let the sun stand still for divine Horus.

We cried out in prayer to great Ra, and begged that the mariners in his Sun Boat of a Million Years ceased to row, so that mighty Ra moved not in his firmament until Horus was better. And indeed time was stopped for all gods and mortals of the universe.

Now my uncle Thoth, who was in the sun-boat at the time, stepped from it and appeared in our company. The great keeper of time, the god of wisdom and magic, had witnessed our divine intervention. Time, of which he is keeper, had been unlawfully stopped by we three in our desperation. Yet he was not angry; for with these words did he cure my son. It has since become a famous healing for a scorpion sting, which is why I repeat it here, so all who hold dear this blessed inscription may save their loved ones from such a tragedy as mine.

A Spell to Cure the Sting of a Scorpion

O GODDESS ISIS, whose lips know
   how to incant charms
No suffering shall befall your child Horus.
May his heart be strong.
The life of Horus is the will of mighty Ra,
He who is in the sun-disk, great creator and
   king of heaven.
His sun-boat is motionless until Horus is
   recovered,
The land lies thirsty and the wells run dry.
By your spirit are you protected oh Horus
The poison is dead, its life in your body withers
Horus lives to the delight of Isis.
And so it shall be for every one who
   possesses these, my words.

THE COBRA GODDESS

Wadjet, the cobra-goddess, is rewarded in the Osiris and Isis myth by being invested with the red crown of Lower Egypt. She is the protector of Horus, the pharaoh-to-be, along with the vulture-goddess Nekhbet. Together they were known as the Two Ladies of the Pharaoh. She was believed to have created the papyrus swamps (and perhaps the papyrus plant itself) that hid Isis and Horus from Set (see page 81). Pharaohs wore the symbol of the red cobra on their heads as a symbol of her protection. The Egyptian Book of the Dead states that Wadjet "...rises upon your head during every hour of the day, even as she does for her father Ra, and through her the terror which you inspire in the spirits is increased... she will never leave you..." Her protective duties continued into the afterlife, as the cobra can be seen on the death mask of Tuthankhamun.

Wadjet was also associated with the lion and the Eye of Ra (see page 39), as daughter of Atum-Ra, who created her as his watchful eyes. By the late period, Wadjet had another sacred animal, the ichneumon. This creature was similar to a mongoose, reputed to destroy snakes and crocodile eggs. According to the Pyramid Texts, the goddess was worshipped at the Temple of Wadjet, or Pe-Dep.

And so it was that clever Thoth blew the sweet breath of existence into my child, just as he had aided me in raising the body of Osiris. Because of this, my devotion to my uncle was great in my heart. I prostrated myself before him, spilling tears of joy and gratitude at his feet. His final words were a warning that there was still much to be done. We had won back the mortal life of Horus and eternal life for Osiris, but Horus was still to wrest the power of the two crowns from Set. Thoth spoke: "This child shall be watched over by his mother, and by the cobra-goddess Wadjet until he takes the rightful throne of his father." With that, the wise god by magic flew back to the firmament. His parting gift to me was the presence of Wadjet, who guarded little Horus whenever I could not be at his side. Now I was content to see him grow into a young man, pride of my existence.

TRANSFORMATIONS —FOR— GOOD AND BAD

TRANSFORMATION BY MAGIC IS A READY FOIL FOR DECEPTION AND DECEIT, BUT MAY ALSO BE USED FOR THE GREATEST MAGIC AND PROTECTION, AS YOU SHALL SEE. NOW GODS AND GODDESSES HAVE ALWAYS BEEN POSSESSED OF THE POWER TO TRANSFORM THE KHAT, THE PHYSICAL FORM, INTO WHATEVER MANNER OF BEAST THEY DESIRE. I HAVE MOSTLY PREFERRED THE SEMBLANCE OF A GREAT BIRD, WHICH IS WHY I AM OFT DEPICTED WITH GREAT WINGS SPREAD ABOUT MY SLENDER FORM. ALL PHARAOHS KNEW ME AS THEIR MOTHER, AND INSCRIBED MY IMAGE THROUGHOUT THEIR KINGDOMS.

MY SON HORUS was now almost grown, and the land of Egypt saw this. So his hardships and victories began in earnest. He began to know of his destiny and to aspire to the power that was just out of his reach.

His first battle, unsurprisingly, was with my brother Set. We two, Horus and I, were to travel to an island delta to meet with the Nine Gods of Heliopolis, when Horus would be introduced to his strange and fearsome family. From the delta to the island, the ferryman Anty steered us where awaited the semblances of gods Shu, Tefnut, Geb, Nut, Thoth, Horus the Elder, Nephthys and Set, and shining Ra.

I trembled as I made my opening gambit. "I am Isis, speaker of spells and namer of names; beloved of Osiris and mother to Horus, our son. I am the deposed queen of the Two Lands," I announced, pausing for effect, "and now I seek justice for my only son, who is cheated of his birthright." I cast a glare at my arrogant and loathed brother Set. "There is one god who sits amongst you whom I openly accuse of unlawful murder, of the attack on a child, of the dismemberment of a god, and the enslavement of my person and that of my sister, Nephthys." All was still as I said these words.

"I accuse, yet truly it is not my proper place to accuse; for that right belongs to my son alone, in the name of his father Osiris, the rightful king of all Egypt." Horus then stood before the assembly, his smaller voice ringing out to claim his power. Set watched coldly, his eyes glinting with malice.

"You are in truth a murderer of men and gods," proclaimed Horus, turning to Set. "You imprisoned my mother when I was but small inside her; by magic you infected me with scorpion-venom; you cast us out of your home so we lived as beggars. But we survive against your will. Not so my father, whom you tricked into his own death and strived to obliterate his name and soul for eternity."

Horus then sat but did not shake as I did. The company was divided; some thought Set a strong ruler, but all could see the rightfulness of Horus' claim to power. Of course Set had no bone of compromise in his body.

"The boy Horus is but young, and in Set we have firm rule," conceded Ra. "Why does Set not keep the throne until the rightful heir comes to manhood? For we know that our present king may have no other heir."

Ra said this because Set was barren. His wanderlust had brought him many mistresses, but none could bear his offspring.

"I will never rescind my rule," cried Set, raging at great Ra and shining Horus. "You will simply prove to me that you deserve my throne." As a plan formed in Set's mind, the flame of his anger cooled. And at that moment he became more dangerous than he had ever been.

"Let us transform our earthly khats into those of hippopotami," he mused. "We will submerge ourselves in water; the first to surface for air will relinquish his claim."

Now Horus readily consented, as did the assemblage; for the burden of responsibility was lifted, and an outcome would be swift.

We walked in readiness to the island's edge, by the reed-clumps where the hippopotami bask. Horus and Set then waded into the muddy waters, summoning up their divine powers of transfiguration. Shortly, only two hippopotami were visible, their new forms casting two marble-like arcs over the horizon. Warily they turned to one another, and slowly sank beneath the water.

Now these two being gods had the ability to transfigure their mortal bodies into hippopotami, just as they might use this power to change into any reptile or beast. Here is a spell for transforming oneself into any shape or form. It tells of a bird, but the bird in flight is the journey of the changeling, the road he must travel before taking his new form. I include it here as I am fond of the metaphor.

SPELL FOR BEING TRANSFORMED INTO ANY SHAPE

I HAVE PASSED BY the Palace
  and it was a bird that brought you to me.
Hail, oh bird, you who flew up to the sky,
The white and shining bird who protects the White Crown.
I shall be with you and I will join the great god;
Make a way for me so I may pass through.

I CONTINUE WITH MY TALE.

The gods and their minions departed but I remained. I could not leave my Horus, as suspected Set of more trickery; when Set was calm it was a sure sign of deception. Little was I to know that my maternal instinct would go so awry. And so I guarded the bank of the island as a huntress, armed with a bow.

For five days and nights I waited by the still waters, primed to spring the first arrow into the heart of Set. As my nerves were as taut as my bow, I sent a death-dart into the first form that raised its head, thinking it to be my vile enemy. Surely enough the beast reared in agony but to my horror I knew it was that of Horus; in panic I withdrew the arrow, and his thrashing form re-entered the waters, just as Set rose to meet my second arrow. This time, the gods were merciful and my arrow struck true. I silently thanked my protectors, while all the time bellowing Set, beast that he was, lumbered through to mud toward me. At my feet he begged and pleaded for his life. I raised my bow, ready to kill him.

"Is not our blood-tie greater than all this?" he pleaded. "Oh sister, I am but weak so do not strike me now."

I must confess my anger drained and I hesitated, a million thoughts rushing through me. My body followed my doubt and my hand, unguided by my head, fell to the ground. In an instant, Set called upon his power and transformed himself back to mortal form as Horus emerged, too transformed, at my side.

HIS ANGER SHOCKED ME DEEPLY.

"Why did you not slay him?" he cried. "You could have saved me from oblivion, yet you let our enemy live on." And with that he drew back his sword, his face contorted in fear and frustration. At that very moment, I knew the meaning of betrayal. Wily Set had always been my familial poison, yet this outrage, and from my own son? I had given my life for him, always, and I now trembled as he was poised to take it for himself.

And his very words turned me to stone. For when his sword cut my neck and separated me from my body I felt nothing. My headless statue crashed to the earth and the arms of my father Geb; my spirit flew to the great arc of sky that is my mother Nut.

THERE WAS NO MORTAL TRACE OF GREAT ISIS.

Here is a spell that may have been inspired by my fate at the hands of my son. The deceased would have needed to study it when living, so taking this knowledge with them to the realm of the underworld, that of my dear Osiris. Of course any mortal needing it would be a truly unfortunate soul, but some may have spoken it for the purposes of calming hysteria.

Now I recall lying motionless with a stilled stone heart, where Horus had severed my head from my body. In rage he fled to the hills, pursued by Thoth, Ra and Set, who had discovered my fallen body. Set was of course inclined to avenge my pathetic state for the sole purpose of proving his power and humiliating my deluded son. Naturally, it was he who found Horus in a sleep of exhaustion in a ravine. Set leapt over the mountains and swooped down on his prey, attacking Horus ferociously. He gouged out his poor eyes and deserted him, then took his prize, along with my head and body of stone, to great Ra. Ra and Thoth then with words of power resurrected me, and I lived and breathed again.

A SPELL FOR KEEPING ONE'S HEAD

I AM GREAT, the son of one who is great
I am a flame, the son of a flame
To whom was given his head after it had
    been cut off.
The head of Osiris will not be taken
    from him
And my head shall not be taken from me.
I am joined together, in justice and youth,
For indeed I am Osiris
The Lord of Eternity.

HIGH IN THE MOUNTAINS, MY SON LAY BLOODIED AND BLIND.

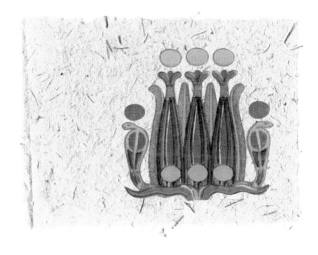

THE HEALING
— OF THE —
EYES

THIS SPELL I REMEMBER VIVIDLY, BECAUSE IT WAS CAST WHEN THE JOY-GODDESS HATHOR FELL IN LOVE WITH MY SON HORUS. IT WAS SURELY PROOF OF THIS GODDESS'S DEVOTION TO HIM, AND A TRUE SIGN THAT SHE WOULD FOLLOW MY MAGICAL PATH, FOR SHE BECAME GODDESS OF LOVE AND HEALING. TO THIS DAY HER HEALING POWER IS SHOWN BY HER COW-HORNS ON HER HEADDRESS, ALTHOUGH SHE CURED NOT BY MEANS OF A COW, BUT BY THE MILK OF ANOTHER BEAST.

This is how Hathor found Horus: she had loved him from afar for many seasons, and decided it was time to pursue him. Guided by her instinct and fascination from afar, she set about searching for him in the great wilderness. Yet instead of bowing before a shining deity, Hathor uncovered a man in agony, whose blood ran the length of the ravine. Immediately she put her arms about him and vowed to heal him. In so doing, she used her magic to capture a gazelle and took its milk, with which she bathed the sockets of his eyes. And as Ra himself created, so Hathor spirited new eyes from the darkness of him, and his sight returned. I therefore dedicate this ritual to her, although of course I am satisfied that it is named after great Isis. Mortals do employ it as a cure for all sickness.

HATHOR, GODDESS OF BEAUTY

Like Isis, hathor is known by many names, which denote her long history in myth and secular worship. She is the goddess of love, music, beauty, dance, women, fertility, children, and childbirth, amongst others. She is depicted carrying a sistrum (a percussion instrument) as a symbol of her playfulness. Temples to her exist in her native country, but she was also known throughout West Asia, particularly in Byblos – where Isis discovered the body of Osiris (see page 61). There is also evidence of Hathor in Ethiopia, Libya, and Somalia. Her province in Egypt, however, was Sinai, the domain of Horus. She was associated with metals, copper, turquoise, and malachite. In Sinai there were malachite mines, and malachite was ground into eye make-up – so adorning the eyes with primitive eye-liner was a way to worship the beauty of Hathor. Her image also decorated mirrors, and she was considered the ruler of perfumiers. Two of her symbols are the abundant cow, and the sycamore – perhaps due to the milky substance emitted by the tree - linking to her role in mythology when she restores Horus' sight with milk.

THE MILK OF ISIS

TAKE THE MILK of a woman who has borne a male child, and drink it.

THIS IS NOT as simple as it sounds. Over the seasons, the people of the Two Lands came up with a cunning solution, using a beautiful clay bottle made in my womanly shape. Milk from a goat or ass was poured into this vessel, then poured out into a cup and drunk. In this way the milk had touched all that was healing, so in turn were they touched by my healing power.

Here too is an invocation to beautiful Hathor, for your amusement, yet mortals do call upon her divine healing using this ritual, and for when they want her beauty, perhaps. An image of the goddess is made in the form of a picture, then this spell is recited by it.

SPELL FOR BEAUTY AND HEALING

❶ HATHOR, Lady of the West;
She of the West; Lady of the Sacred
    Land;
Eye of Ra, which is on his forehead;
Kindly of countenance in the Sun Boat of
    a Million Years;
A resting-place for him who has done right
    within the boat of the blessed;
Who built the great barque of Osiris in
    order to cross the water of truth.

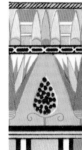

Hathor then took Horus, now healed, to the court of Heliopolis, again to confront Set and claim his rightful throne. Set, I think must have had some secret knowledge of Hathor's healing which he passed on to Ra; maybe I am mistaken. Yet Ra's condemnation that followed was surely telling.

"Isis, your treachery is unmistakeable, and your own son has punished you for it," he pronounced (little did he know that my punishment was due to my weak-heartedness in not killing Set.) "The red god Set wins the contest and throne for you, Horus, are unworthy."

"But how can this be true?" Horus retorted. "I will never bow before your ruling." And then came the blow. "You are a child, still with the milk of your mother in your mouth, smothered by women. You have no place here." And with that he turned from Horus, dismissing him, as the court fell silent at Ra's vicious attack.

Hathor again came to Horus' aid, and transformed the rage of the great father. Hathor, beautiful goddess of desire, presented her body to him naked so that his fast fury turned to desire. With her deferential charm she appeased his pride; and in due course he agreed to hold court to Horus and Set once more, and again rule on their dual claim.

On The Division
— of the —
Dead and the Living

Never shall these two states be entwined, for with it comes the chaos of the universe, and all creation must again begin. Those who live and rule must not meddle with the realm of the underworld, for it has its own rites and rules for living in death. And those who dwell in eternity must not have sway over the constitution of kings and pharaohs.

The truth of this rule was to be the unravelling of the knot of discord that plagued the Two Lands as Horus and Set feuded in bitterness over the crowns of Egypt.

For seasons their battles, both petty and bloody, afflicted the equilibrium of the company of gods. In the absence of no otherworldly solution Thoth, god of words, asked for the opinion of Osiris in the form of a letter. For was not his lineage the source of this discontent? Thoth's entreaty to the god of the underworld was despatched, with the full blessing of Ra.

Many days later, Osiris' reply came into the hands of Ra. It was both an opinion and a warning. Sighing, Ra read from the papyrus: "I dwell here with Maat, she who is truth and justice. Your goodness is great, yet I cannot rest until my son is given all he deserves. Know that my power is greater than yours; know that I have been patient; and so believe I will take the truth of Maat and together we will demand the divine right of my son to be king."

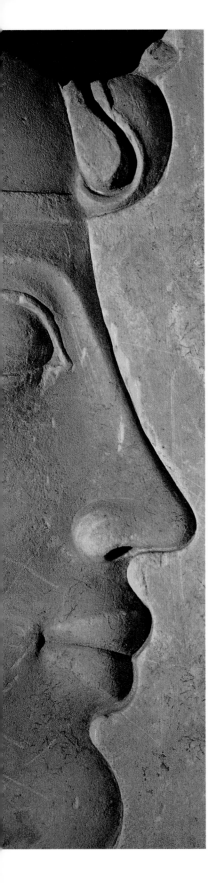

Ra shone the light of his august radiance onto Thoth, and declared, "Now this is too much; it cannot be that Osiris of the underworld may challenge my power. If the realm of the dead and realm of the living mingle, only destruction can ensue. This is my domain, and I will rule it." Now when I heard this I truly believed that Ra was to thwart poor Horus. I have to say I was surprised and delighted with the outcome.

"Let Horus be brought before me." My son was duly summoned and brought before the shining one. He cast his radiance over Horus, who knelt at his golden feet. He then proclaimed him king of the Two Lands, and bestowed upon him the red and white crowns of Egypt, and the crook and flail of kingship, proving him the supreme ruler of the land. His two protectors were summoned, great Wadjet, the cobra of the north (who as you may remember used to mind him as a child) and Nekhebet, vulture of the south.

Horus then spoke to his father Osiris in tearful homage. "O lord of gods, who dwells in right and truth, behold me; your son Horus, comes before you," he began. "I have avenged you, and brought you Maat, even here, within the company of gods. Grant that I may live among those who worship you, for I have overthrown all your enemies, and have kept all those who are of you upon the earth for ever and ever." As Horus turned his face to the assemblage, he had the true semblance of his father upon him, and shone with his beauty. For all we had sacrificed was rewarded.

Set, in fury, turned upon mighty Ra. From that day on his warrior-armies roamed the land, thirsty for the blood of Horus. To overturn the Boat of a Million Years they shifted their shapes into crocodiles and hippopotami; in the delta marshes close by his city of Avaris, Set transformed his followers into beasts of the river, lying in wait for the flotilla of Ra. In each feud and skirmish they were overcome; yet Set always escaped, ever wily. With this in mind, I introduce here for your amusement a little ritual thought to have been used by mortals who suffered during the ongoing conflict. At one time it was employed also as a love-trick, but it reminds me so of my enslavement by my brother Set, so I do not recommend it for these purposes.

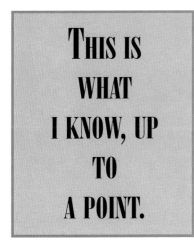

THIS IS WHAT I KNOW, UP TO A POINT.

SPELL TO RESTRAIN AN ENEMY

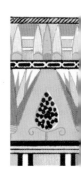

MADE OF A MIXTURE of wax, pitch, and gum, the figure of the enemy. To be formed in a kneeling position, with the hands tied behind the back.

Made of the same concoction, the figure of the opponent who desires victory. To be formed in a standing position, holding a sword at the throat of the enemy.

The names of demons are written on the figure of the enemy.

With thirteen needles of bronze the limbs of the enemy are pierced and these words are spoken:

I pierce the (saying the name of the limb) that my enemy be restrained from bringing me harm.

Special words of power were inscribed onto a metal plate, which was then tied to the wax figures with a string bearing three hundred and sixty-five knots. The entire amulet was then buried in the grave of a young person, or of someone who had died violently.

These are extreme measures and in truth may consort too greatly with the idea of death rather than the healing of ills. So here I present something lighter in tone; talking of violence brings back too keenly the painful memories of my past.

HOW TO WALK UPON YOUR ENEMY

WRITE THE NAME of the enemy on the soles of both the sandals that you wear daily. Or, inscribe a symbol or image of them, using black ink alone or with color. Let the words and image dry, and think upon your enemy. Now, walk upon the earth with the knowledge that you tread them underfoot.

What is agreed is that my beloved son became pharaoh and ruled with justice; what is debatable is the final combat between Horus and Set. According to some mortals, Horus punished him so that he dragged his screaming form before Ra (although none had seen this, due to the great clouds of dust thrown up during their fighting. I would like to think that my earth-god father, Geb, had a hand in this.) Then Ra told Horus to take Set to me, great Isis, so I would have the final say on his fate. Legend has it that I took ultimate revenge, slicing off Set's head and limbs and casting every part of him over the lands of Egypt, just as he had mutilated the body of my beloved Osiris. Others avow that this final battle did not take place, and prophesy that it will happen at the end of the world, when Osiris returns to the earth.

The truth of this is a mystery to those who walk the earth, but know this: the mercy of Isis extends to all, save one.

FOR HIM I RESERVE JUST RETRIBUTION.

5 THE SPELLS OF LOVE AND SEDUCTION

OF PURRING AND PASSION,

OF CLAWS AND CATS

AND OF THE SEDUCTIVE CHARMS

OF THE FELINE-PRIESTESSES

OF BUBASTIS, OF THEIR

MANY SPELLS FOR LOVE AND

SOME OF

MY OWN.

BEAUTY AND BAST

Lᴏɴɢ ᴀɢᴏ, ɪɴ ᴍʏ ᴛɪᴍᴇ ᴏғ ᴡᴀɴᴅᴇʀɪɴɢs, ᴡʜᴇɴ I sᴏᴜɢʜᴛ ᴛʜᴇ ᴘᴏᴏʀ sᴜɴᴅᴇʀᴇᴅ ʀᴇᴍᴀɪɴs ᴏғ ᴍʏ ʙᴇʟᴏᴠᴇᴅ Osɪʀɪs, I ᴅᴡᴇʟᴛ ғᴏʀ ᴀ ᴛɪᴍᴇ ɪɴ ᴛʜᴇ sᴜʟᴛʀʏ Dᴇʟᴛᴀ ᴄɪᴛʏ ᴏғ Bᴜʙᴀsᴛɪs, ᴛʜᴇ ᴘʟᴀᴄᴇ ᴡʜᴇʀᴇ ᴛʜᴇ ᴄᴀᴛ ɪs ᴡᴏʀsʜɪᴘᴘᴇᴅ, ᴀɴᴅ ᴛʜᴇ ɢᴏᴅᴅᴇss Bᴀsᴛ ʜᴏʟᴅs sᴡᴀʏ.

Bᴀsᴛ (who happens to be an aunt of mine) is said to be an insatiable lover, whose antics have long been the subject of controversy for all those who ride in the sky-boat of Rᴀ. Be that as it may, the people of her city share many of the amorous characteristics of their cat-goddess, whom they believe to be the very image of love itself. After all, she is beautiful, playful and affectionate, hunting the night for a mate. Yet she can spit and possesses wicked claws to rend a heart in two.

The priestesses of Bᴀsᴛ are likewise noted for their beauty, and sometimes for their cruelty in love-play. They are adept at luring the man they desire to their beds when the moon rides high. However, if their physical allure proves insufficient to the task, these harlot priestesses are prepared to resort to a spell of seduction to remedy the situation and win the man of their desires. If you are a man intoxicated with a woman and want to win her for your own, say the Song of the Wild Goose. Speak these spells when the moon is full, and the man or woman you desire will come to you.

In exquisite Bubastis I saw the necessity to put my sorrow aside for a short while and there learned much strange love-magic from my aunt. She whispered to me at night of elixirs and potions, rituals and lotions; as I lay in restless sleep she purred to me, of perfumery, seduction and feline charm. As with all aunts, she little realized the life I had truly seen and my enduring

THE SONG OF THE CAT

IF I AM NOT with you, where will you go?
If good fortune comes your way, you still
   cannot find happiness.
But if you come to touch my breasts and
   thighs, then will you be satisfied at last.
Because you remember you are hungry,
   still you would not leave.
Are you a man who thinks only of his stomach?
You would not walk from me in your finery
   and leave me with but a sheet.
Because of hunger you would not leave me!
Because of thirst you would not leave me!
Take my breast, for you its gift overflows!
Better indeed is one day in my arms than a
   hundred thousand anywhere on earth.

THE SONG OF THE WILD GOOSE

DISTRACTING IS THE foliage of my
   pasture
The mouth of my girl is a lotus bud
Her breasts are mandrake apples
Her arms are vines
Her eyes are fixed like berries
Her brow a snare of willow
And I the wild goose.

love for Osiris; so by the third night of my stay, when I was mortally sick of her entreaties, I took myself out of my dwelling.

Now at that time I was little more than a wandering shadow, and my anonymity afforded me blessed disguise. Isis in spirit was dim, but my plain body carried me toward the infinite temple of Bast. If the ferocious goddess so invaded my dreams, then why should I not invade her sanctum? For know that at this time, during my lost years, I had neither peace nor comfort from the painful loss of Osiris. And I confess that as I walked, a shroud of sadness clouded my heart. The sweet music that drifted from even the meanest dwellings turned to a lonely envy in my mind. And at each twist and turn of the walkway was I observed by my aunt's little watchers of the night: shrines of tiny cats, their crescent eyes glinting like the stars of the celestial Nile. Never failing to follow the sweep of my cloak as I meandered by the black waters of that island city.

By the headland the river flashed with myriad oil lamps, their flames spitting pungent incense. And at the end of this avenue of night-suns lay the most beautiful building, set by a gold pylon and guarded by the dark forms of two great cats, hewn from onyx. I admit I stood in awe and let my fingers reach out and touch the statues. They felt like cool glass to my fingers and reminded me of the finery of my father's house in Heliopolis. To a stranger, I must have cast a sad figure; a beggar woman feeling the smooth, sleek beauty of a cat, lost in her memories.

So to the inner sanctum of Bast, for this was my aunt's true resting place. At her feet all mortals laid their tiny mummified cats, in jars of oil; and there too they spoke love-prayers and asked for her blessings. And I was sure to give her no rest that night, for I intended to tell of all my woes by that potent shrine of desire.

ALL WAS DESERTED AND STILL.

I looked to the bejeweled beauty of the shrine and saw that by the censer was a singular papyrus scroll. I confess that like the cats that ever surrounded me in this sultry place I was drawn to it by an unbearable curiosity. The ink was fresh; I looked about me and turned my eye to its content. For inscribed were all manner of magical formulae and equations, and cunning rituals to harness the power of love and evoke the wiles of the feline goddess.

I spoke the first spell to myself in a quiet murmur. Now I would like to believe that it was meant for me, as at other such times have I been rescued from the doldrums. As uncle Thoth, god of scribes, had stolen days from the moon to give me birth, now he conspired with aunt Bast. For before my eyes was a spell for the passion of Osiris; and the reason I had come to this odd sanctuary was in my hands.

Here is why I know this spell to be efficacious. When the body of Osiris was torn apart by my evil brother, I gathered up his poor remains excepting his phallus, which had been consumed by an oxyrhynchus fish. I surely think that the taking of this fish for a love-potion makes mortals call upon the potency of Osiris; for even without his this true appendage did he give me my longed-for child. My aunt, however, disagrees. To seduce a priestess of Bast, she says, a fish is perfect, for all cats do love it.

THE PASSION OF OSIRIS

THE OXYRHYNCHUS, a fish of the Nile, burned to charcoal
The oil of roses, or the pulp of rose petals

THE NILE-FISH is to be ground to black dust and the rose-oil is mingled with it, to give a paste. The man daubs his head with this unguent, and all women shall then want him. Now if the oxyrhynchus fish cannot be found, another fish of the Nile is employed. Or, the spittle of a stallion can be collected and with it the man anoints his phallus, and lies with the woman. Now I have heard from my aunt Bast that the spittle makes the woman reach her greatest ecstasy. Yet whosoever gleans the stallion-spittle is seen by all in the city, for one must go abroad into the daylight and be espied near the horses by the market. And men, being of nature proud, do dislike others knowing of their need for sex-magic.

BAST, THE CAT-GODDESS

Cat-goddess Bast was also known as Bastet and to the Greeks, who, strangely considered her to be a virgin, Artemis. An alternative name was pesht – the origin of "puss." Bast's cult center was at Bubastis (modern-day Tell Basta, north of Giza) which came to prominence during the rule of the Libyan pharaoh Sheshon I, in the middle of the tenth century BCE. As Bubastis was his residence, the city and its principal goddess Bast rose to fame and prominence within the Egyptian pantheon. Miwsher, meaning "little cat" or "pussycat," became a popular nickname for Egyptian girls.

Bast was portrayed as a cat, or as a woman with the head of her sacred animal. She had a reputation for ferocity, as a protector from demons and disease. Her gentler side was as the sensuous deity of music, pleasure, dance, and fertility. Her feminine qualities associate her with Hathor. Bast may have been another form of that goddess or considered to be her sister, and as the possible daughter of Isis. Such is the nature of the convoluted family relationships of the gods of Old Egypt. Festivals at her hometown of Bubastis, recorded by Herodotus, were held during April and May when the citizens took to sailing boats, singing and playing drums. Bast figurines often show her holding a sistrum, an ancient Egyptian percussion instrument. The sistrum provides another link to Hathor, a goddess with whom Bast shares many attributes. This musical instrument was considered to be the sacred symbol of laughing Hathor, patroness of passion and drunkenness.

And so I settled myself by the velvet paws of great Bast to read on. The next spell on the papyrus confused me. I did not comprehend fully the magical inscription, and at first thought it bore harm to the memory of Osiris; but on reflection it was only love-torment, and this was close to my own heart. What of the poor mortal who had need of it? In the name of the sunboat of shining Ra, why did mortals and gods suffer so? Could it be that the reason is that we were born of the tears of that mighty god? Forgive me, for I get ahead of myself. I will now tell of how the incantation of the second spell came about.

As I perused the papyrus script I started at the sound of a footfall and spun around in shock. In truth I could be discovered and cast out of that sweet sanctuary, a beggar woman; and if I had been caught with the papyrus then I would be doubly exposed, as no peasant could read nor write his own name. I waited and watched, my breath came fast and my heart raced; a heady scent hung heavy in the inky black of the sanctum. I knew that I was being observed, and not solely by the all-seeing eyes of Bast. The aroma of roses stung my senses, sharp and imploring.

ALL WAS SILENT, BUT I WAITED. FOR PATIENCE IS ONE OF MY CERTAIN VIRTUES.

"Oh goddess, I entreat you, listen to me!" I gasped as a voice without form rang out. Then before me stepped a youth so beautiful; not as Osiris you understand, but as an exquisite soldier of the gods; strong and muscular, with eyes the color of the Great Green Sea.

"How did you know of me?" I cried in exasperation. For if I reveal myself as Isis I do so at my choosing, and not at the whim of a mere mortal. Even though he was perfect to look upon.

"O great Isis, my name is Pe-fera, born of the sculptress Nemar; I dreamed of you and your aunt Bast; and my fate is to come to this temple this very night. I am in such a torment of love." At that he knelt before me, a man who looked like a god prostrate before a goddess with the semblance of a beggar. I touched the crown of his head in blessing and through my fingertips came the unspoken story of his unrequited passion. He had no more words to tell but he needed them not. For through my touch alone I knew he must have the woman he loved; and that the papyrus spell, which I repeat here, was his love-cure.

I took his lovely face and tilted his chin toward me. I looked into Pe-fera's pained eyes with compassion; for no other god or mortal walking the earth should suffer as I had. "Come," I instructed him calmly, "this very incantation was put in my hands for you." And so I read to him the spell of the Flame of Love. As I did so, I added the name of his beloved, Nemer, to make my words live.

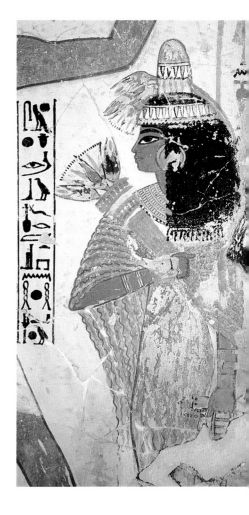

THE FLAME OF LOVE

HAIL TO THEE, O Ra-Harakhte, Father of the Gods!
Hail to you, O seven Hathors
Who are adorned with strings of red thread!
Hail to you, yet Gods, lords of heaven and earth!
Come make Nemer, born of Ehkmer, come after me,
Like an ox after grass,
Like a servant after her children
Like a drover after his herd!
If you do not make her come after me,
Then I will set fire to Busiris [Abydos] and burn up Osiris.

I CONFESS, being fond of the youth, I taught him a trick of love divination to go with it, so that if he were ever to cast a love spell again he would know its potential and potency in advance of the affair. So here is Pe-fera's little ritual by which I hope that he will remember me.

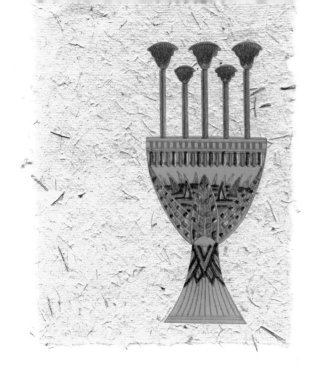

The Prophesy of the Dog

Now the following are gathered together.

A figure of a dog eight fingers long, made from wax and gum

A tablet of lead

A tripod or platform, small in height

Magical words are written on the figure of the dog where the ribs are. Now this may be the question in mind. On the lead tablet, the names of demons are inscribed, for it is they who must assist in the ritual. The tripod is placed on the tablet; the dog is placed on the tripod; and all the words on the tablet and the dog are recited. If the dog snarls, the spell will fail. If the dog barks, it will be a success and the love-wish will come true.

For those of you that need distraction from thinking about the torments of love, or would seek solace when melancholy yearnings govern your heart, here is a love story of sorts for your perusal. I considered the discovery of this yarn to be like the finding of a rare jewel at the bottom of the ocean. Like a many-colored, beautiful yet elusive fish, the jewel represents love but it may be any deep love that lies beneath the surface. To my mind finding this treasure is that which restores the heart: it is faith, or the wisdom of Thoth, or the light or Ra, returning like a long-lost child after a seeming age of darkness.

It began with the low spirits of king Seneferu which cast gloom over his days and plunged his nights into an agonising depth of melancholy. This king longed for that which would lift his heart; a distraction of love and light pleasure, or some other spectacle that befitted the restlessness of a ruler. So he commanded that his high priest Tchatcha-em-ankh be brought into his presence, for the very name of this magus spoke of the magic of life itself.

"My nobles have not the means to cheer me; they have tempted me with all at their disposal, yet my melancholy shadows me day and night," sighed Seneferu. "What is to be done?"

And Tchatcha-em-ankh replied: "Take to the lake, O sovereign; for I will commission a royal boat, furnished with the comforts of the palace; and twenty beautiful maidens, each with an exquisite paddle of ebony and gold, shall row you.

"From the boat," he continued, "you will see the beauty of your earthly paradise: the thickets of the lake, the lush fields of your domain. And your heart will gladden at the sight of all you have created."

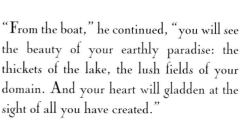

THE EGYPTIAN HEART

The heart was believed to be the emotional and spiritual center of the body, and was treated with utmost care after death. The hieroglyph for "heart" is a two-handled urn, in which the heart was preserved as part of the funerary ritual. A scarab amulet (see page 15) was laid on the body in place of the heart, and spells recited so that the bearer would gain entry into the afterlife. These incantations were needed, because the deceased's heart would be weighed against the feather of truth (symbolic of Maat) at the gates. If he or she had committed crimes, their hearts would be heavy; those unburdened by misdeeds would pass through the gate. The Egyptian Book of the Dead includes a number of spells that express this belief.

"My heart, my mother; my heart, my mother!
My heart whereby I came into being!
May naught stand up to oppose me at [my] judgment;
may there be no opposition to me in the presence of the sovereign princes;
may there be no parting of thee from me...
Let there by joy of heart unto us at the weighing of words
Let not that which is false be uttered against me
before the great god, the lord of Amentet . . ."

This came to be when the sun-boat of Ra next rose in his glory over the horizon. The maidens were given their paddles and sat naked in nets, like rare, alluring urchins of the deep. There they rowed, all overseen by wise Tchatcha-em-ankh, who directed the course of the boat through the jade waters, and truly the path of the king's malaise. At every stroke of the oars did his joy return.

That was, until the maiden who took the prow flatly refused to row any more. She lay down her paddle and as she did so, all the other maidens followed her lead. The boat drifted, and the head maiden would not continue.

"Why do you not row for me?" inquired the king. "And why must all your company cease in their endeavor?"

"I have lost my jewel of new turquoise from my hair," she retorted. "My paddle entangled in my tresses, and I pulled it free. Yet now my precious stone has fallen into the water, and I can row for you no more."

TCHATCHA-EM-ANKH STROKED HIS CHIN AND PONDERED THE SITUATION.

"I will return it to you," he promised and with that, the priest and scribe spoke certain magical words of Heka to the waters of the lake. I trust he implored great Nun to aid him, the deity of the watery chaos that was the universe before my coming. And at his order the lake rose on one side, like the wall of a mighty temple with form as solid as rock. It was twelve cubits deep. I do believe this priest to have had a high calling for magic, for he must have had the ability to evoke mighty Ra to make time stand still.

Tchatcha-em-ankh then glimpsed the turquoise amulet on the bed of the lake, a dot of vibrant blue on a vast marsh. He took it in his hand and gave it to the maiden, then commanded that the waters return to their natural state. With more words of power, the strange wall of water was restored to its proper place and resumed a glassy calm.

As for Seneferu and the stubborn maiden, well she was no maiden shortly after because by attracting the notice of the king she also enticed His Majesty into love, a law higher then any he could decree. She was his wife thereafter and long did they live in happiness proving that love is a fit foe for all melancholy. I think Tchatcha-em-ankh planned the whole thing.

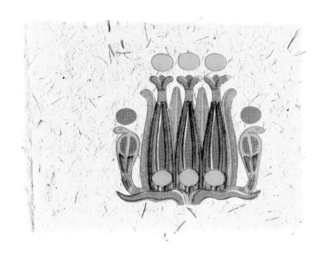

Magic demands great risk, and as love is truly the mightiest kind of magic, so it is inevitably a risk to the soul. And if true love cannot be found, then all else stops, as the maidens must stop rowing until love is found again. Here is a spell to gain your true love from the depths of the heart.

The Song of the Red Fish

Speak aloud this incantation, for it was inscribed on a vase at Memphis and dedicated I think to my daughter-in-law, beautiful Hathor. Both men and women do send requests such as this to the goddess, pleading their love-cause so that she may bless them.

I love to go and bathe before you
I allow you to see my beauty
in a dress of the finest linen
drenched with fragrant oils.
I go down into the water
to be with you
and come up to you again
with a red fish,
looking splendid upon my fingers.
I offer it to you…
Come! Look at me!

DESIRE — AND — DECEIT

LOVE, AS IT IS EVER OF BEAUTY, CAN BRING THE GREATEST HEARTACHE. INDEED, THE WILY PRIESTESSES OF BAST MAY CHARM AND DESTROY IN EQUAL MEASURE. NOW PE-FERA HAD THE GREAT GOOD FORTUNE TO RECEIVE HEALING, AS I HAD THE GREAT FORTUNE TO GIVE HEALING; FOR HEALING IS A GIFT THAT IS FREELY GIVEN.

Love that is binding is never free. For this dark-natured love does exact dire penalty, which I here I will tell, as gentle warning.

My uncle Thoth's book of magic contains the infinite truth of existence. Indeed this Book of Thoth is so sacred and secret that no man shall come upon it, as he may then take the mantle of a god. So, my clever uncle buried it in its own tomb beneath the waters of the Nile, and had it guarded by a fearsome serpent who coiled his scaly form tight around the tomb, so none should take it.

But prince Setnau, the eleventh son of the great ruler Ramesses II, was schooled in the arts of Heka and of priestly magic, and desired this arcane book of my uncle's more than the throne or his wife. By sorcery did he obtain it; but that is its own tale.

Now the wise and great Ramesses warned his son to leave the Book of Thoth untouched and return it to its rightful resting place. Setnau, being headstrong and too full of his own ambition, hesitated and instead visited the temple of the great architect Ptah, in his city of Memphis. There his eyes alighted on the most sultry creature he had ever witnessed. Sleek and supple, her lips were divine and her eyes piercing; her black tresses swung as she swayed toward the temple, her graceful wrists and neck clad in gold. She stopped to rest not in the shade of the palms, but in the full flame of the sun. And there she basked under the great sky boat of mighty Ra.

Now Setnau was not one to refuse a challenge, as we shall see; and he sent forth a servant to enquire of her. Her name was Tabibu, the daughter of the priest of Bast; and when foolish Setnau offered her gold for an hour of her company in private, she struck a deal. Setnau was to come to her house in sultry Bubastis, where none would know of their liaison.

Setnau, delighted, set out for that delta city, all the while thinking of Tabibu. For he wanted her now more than the Book of Thoth, his foresight clouded by a lust so potent that all else was dust.

I WILL BE BRIEF.

Tabibu entertained Setnau, purring her longing for him yet frustrating him with her diversions. She commanded fine sweetmeats and luscious honey wine, drunk from goblets inlaid with precious minerals; music of love to soothe his senses; and the great perfumes of rose, of oranges, and of lotus.

EGYPTIAN APHRODISIACS

Mandrake apples (see page 47) were thought to be an aphrodisiac. An Arabic name for the plant is devil's testicles, probably as some of its species are shaped like male genitals. Other plants of passion included radish, ginger, and garlic; lettuce was revered for its potent properties, and the variety grown in ancient Egypt was tall and long leaved, emitting a milky substance when squeezed. The lettuce was also associated with the fertility god, Min. The fig was Cleopatra's favorite fruit, thought to promote fertility and a good sex drive. The power of the onion to drive a man or woman wild was also documented – priests were forbidden to eat onions in order to preserve their chastity.

Setnau's longing had now risen to a fever. He watched Tabibu's delicious breasts rise and fall as she idly ordered yet another delicacy, knowing fully his eyes were upon her.

"Come, let us make love now," implored Setnau, reaching toward her.

"Do you really think that I would prostitute myself for your gold?" she teased, "when if you truly wanted me, I would have the rights of a mistress?" So Setnau, love-blind, sent for a scribe. He assigned all his worldly property to Tabibu of Bubastis. And that done, he asked again that they lay together.

"But you have children, great prince," she chided. "And they can have no claim to your estate, surely, for where would I be then? If I am your true love, then you should have no fear of giving me all." At this point Setnau was so lustful he agreed; and he again sent for the scribe, and the papers were drawn up. It was decreed that the children and the half-brother of Setnau would be disinherited from that day forward.

"Now my love," pleaded the prince, "you have my power, my lands; and it is time that I had you."

But tabibu had another surprise.

"I do not want your half-brother or children to make complaint to the pharaoh on my account. Therefore they cannot live, and you must order their execution or we will never lay together."

And it was done.

Fear was his salvation, yet Desire his master.

The feline temptress then took Setnau by the hand to her bed. No thoughts of his family tormented him as he sought the promise of the lips of Tabibu and made to touch her breast. Yet as his fingertip glanced her skin, a scream was rent, so vicious and spitting that the prince covered his ears in pain. Setnau shut his eyes, recoiling at the splintering sound of wood and glass around him. Red and shaking, he looked for Tabibu. But that bed, where all his passion had burned, lay empty; and with a sickening in his heart, Setnau remembered the plight of his children and half-brother, murdered on the whim of a dark stranger.

In the place of tabibu lay the dusty scroll that was the book of thoth.

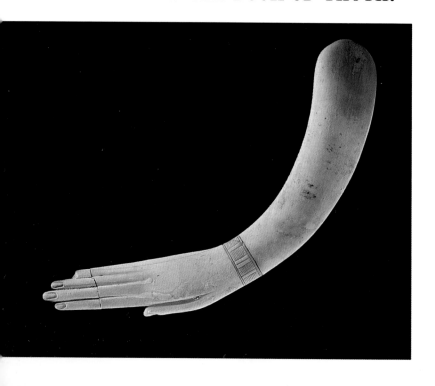

And so the quest for knowledge with avarice is as base as lust. Yet Setnau had only been visited by Tabibu in a demonic dream, and on returning to Memphis found his family safe and well. Needless to say, this experience had so frightened the prince that he returned the book promptly and tried with all his heart never to think on its mysteries again.

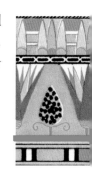

HERE IS A LOVE PROTECTION SPELL.

SPELL TO RESIST TEMPTATION

TAKE A SYMBOL of the Eye of Horus (or of Ra, for it is the same). It affords the wearer inner sight. Place it around the neck as a pendant or, paint it onto the body using vegetable dye. This should be done when the moon is young.

THIS AMULET is worn at all times. When next temptation assails, the Eye is touched to fend off evil intent.

Mortals can use it when they are in danger of being overwhelmed by lust. I inscribe it here because it evokes my beloved son, Horus, and my seductive aunt Bast; for Horus allowed Bast to wear his eye-symbol for him. It is a clever spell for it fights fire with fire. It transforms the malicious feline into the gently purring cat of healing, so the predator is confronted with his or her own dark side. When this is performed successfully, the good is weighed with the bad, which gives a total of naught. So the temptation will surely disappear.

Now as surely as I love balance, I set out here two more spells. One is to invigorate a man; the other is for women who have a sufficiency of children and wish for no more. This is foreign in my sacred land, as all mortals there desire many offspring, but I hear that women of distant lands do use it.

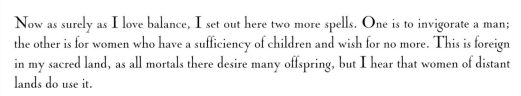

THE ELIXIR OF YOUTH

The Egyptians had their own version of the elixir of youth. It was found written on the reverse of part of the Edwin Smith Surgical Papyrus, which dates from c. 1700 BCE. This papyrus was a copy of the lost papyrus of the Old Kingdom which was attributed to Imhotep, the master priest and architect of the first pyramids of Egypt. To make an old man appear as a youth, a wrinkle cream was concocted from hemayet – a plant with a husk, that is unfortunately untranslatable. It was boiled to make a thick residue then preserved in an expensive stone vase prior to use. When applied to the face, it was claimed to remove blemishes, wrinkles and all signs of aging.

FOR THE POTENCY OF OSIRIS

THIS MAGICAL concoction is both sweet and sour, like love.
The juice of an onion
A spoonful of honey

THE ONION JUICE and honey are to be mixed into an unguent and drunk by the man. He will be fertile for every hour of great Ra and Khonsu.

A SPELL FOR NINE SEASONS

THIS RECIPE is secret and known only by women, I think, as it stops her fertility for three or nine seasons. Acacia dates are taken and stoned. The pulp is crushed and mixed with honey, then the mixture is dipped in wool and placed within her.

6 THE SPELLS OF DIVINATION FOR WHEN I WANTED TO KNOW OF THE FUTURE

WHERE IT IS TOLD OF THE SECRETS OF FORETELLING THE FUTURE WITH FLAMES AND A BOWL OF DIVINATION, AND OF THE SECRETS OF THE STARS AND GODS SHOWN IN THE HOROSCOPE OF ANNU THAT PREDICTS THE DAYS OF GOOD FORTUNE AND BAD.

THE OMEN OF THE FLAMES

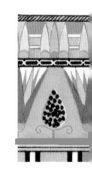

BEFORE MY MARRIAGE TO OSIRIS I HAD MANY
QUESTIONS ABOUT THE FUTURE AND THE PAST.
MY CURIOSITY THEN KNEW NO BOUNDS, TO THE
ANNOYANCE OF MY ELDERS, AND MY HIGH
PRIESTESS, NEFERURE. I KNEW THAT SHE
PRACTICED MANY RITES OF MAGIC, AND I HAD
THE HUNGER FOR IT WELL BEFORE I GAINED THE
POWER OVER ALL CREATION, HAVING ENTICED
MY FEEBLE GREAT FATHER, RA, TO TELL ME
HIS TRUE NAME.

I WOULD LIKE to say that I was taught this divination, but if I am truthful I taught it to myself, having secretly pursued my priestess one day as she fled through the outer pylon to the anteroom by the inner sanctum. I knew that she was trying to catch the rays of mighty Ra and so must have had a mind for magic. I watched close, having hidden myself by the doorway, and noted that she took a white lamp and walked to the eastern wall. From her robes she took a digging tool, and made to gouge a small recess in the wall. She tapped rhythmically, bent to her task.

HER EVERY MOVEMENT WAS MEASURED, AND IN MY STEALTH I DARED NOT BREATHE.

The lamp wick was untouched and fresh. She took a gourd of palm oil and with it filled the lamp, and held it opposite the sun, mighty Ra; and recited the following incantation in praise of Him at his rising. I remember it because she repeated it four times, after which I recited it to myself in my mind again and again until I could write it down on reaching my chamber.

THE INCANTATION TO RA

HAIL TO THEE O Ra in thy rising,
Even to thee who is called Atum at thy dawning.
Yea, great Ra who comes as Khephera, the ever-living.

DIVINATION BY LAMP AND FLAME

The incantation to Ra is found on a papyrus composed in the eighteenth dynasty in the reign of Pharaoh Amenophis III Nebmaatra (1390–1352 BCE). It is unfortunate that the text does not go on to inform one of how the answer to the question is given. However, its similarity to a form of divination called pyromancy may suggest the solution. In this case one need not gouge a hole in a wall, but stand by a window facing east. The pyromantic version of the invocation is as follows:

"Fire, fire, holy fire
Unto fortune I aspired,
I await a sign from thee
That my prayers answered be!"

The invocation to Ra or the above may be used. At this point, take a pinch of powdered frankincense and sprinkle it on the lamp flame as you speak your question. The flame will answer the question as follows:

The answer is "yes" or a good omen if the flame ascends in a thin steady spire or a conical shape with little smoke. It is even better if the flame is silent, neither crackling nor spitting. It is an excellent omen if the flame splits into three prongs.

The answer is "no" or a bad omen for the future if the flame becomes smoky and dark, or does not rise, crackles and spits or splits into two prongs. It is worse if the flame suddenly bends to one side because this warns of impending difficulties and sickness. It is worse still should the flame go out for then you will have earned the enmity of the gods and inevitable disaster will strike. The only hope in this case is to spit at the lamp and curse it with the misfortune that would otherwise fall upon you. If the flame wavers from side to side, then a visit from friends and relatives is to be expected soon.

The Scrying of the Bowl

NOW WHEN I was in my wanderings I rested at the oasis of Siwa, the holy city of the barren wastes of the western desert that was to become the domain of my red brother, Set. My entrance to that forsaken metropolis marked the star-crossed path of my existence; for at this time my mortal life was as barren as the dust that abraded my eyes and seeped through my sandals. Every part of me was swathed in blue linen (for that is my color) in defence of the storming sands; yet as I approached that glittering turquoise oasis, all was calmness itself.

I rested at Siwa a while, to regain my strength after the long journey. Like so many pilgrims, I was lost in a sea of devotees who came there to find what their futures held. The priests at Siwa were great adepts at divining, for at this place was to be found the very core of the future: the oracle of Amun himself, the hidden aspect of mighty Ra.

The temple itself was perfect in all dimensions, as if Ptah himself had made it in his hand and set it down in a grove of lush palms. In the inner sanctum of the temple was a great statue of the god where all – including the great pharaohs – would approach and in secret ask their question. Now the nobles would have easy access to the oracle, they being rulers of high command. Yet some of the common people waited many dawns for an audience, and so Siwa was scattered with every type of mortal. They came from everywhere. Here was a mother who begged Amun for knowledge of the health of her husband; there a youth in a fit of love-sickness; the shaven-headed priests came too from both delta towns and the deep desert to enquire of their magical future. Could it be that they would follow in the lauded footsteps of great Imhotep, that conceiver of the first pyramids and weaver of spells and dreams?

Now even the mortals of Siwa who were unconnected with the temple oracle were superstitious by nature, and could foresee the future by use of a bowl. Here are two of their rituals, for your amusement. It can be dedicated to myself, Isis; Bast, the cat-goddess who is my aunt; or lovely Hathor, my lovely daughter-in-law. Mortals do choose one of us three, for later in my history we all became as one, deities of love, healing, and protection.

A Dream Divination With the Bowl of Isis

A DIVINING, OR SCRYING, bowl is taken, or a simple bowl that has been consecrated for this purpose. It must be made of a substance such as glazed clay or glass and not be harmful and the drinking from it must be safe.

The leaves of the mint-plant or lettuce are crushed, and their green juice is used as ink. Inside the lower part of the bowl, the person inscribes their question to the goddess. Then the name of the goddess is written three times: "Isis, Isis, Isis," or "Hathor, Hathor, Hathor," and so on. Water is then poured into the bowl to cover the inscriptions; and one waits until they are entirely dissolved, and the questions has reached the ears of the goddess.

The water is then drunk and the inquirer goes to sleep. On awakening, he or she will remember a dream in which the answer to the question is given.

SIWA, THE CITY OF ORACLES

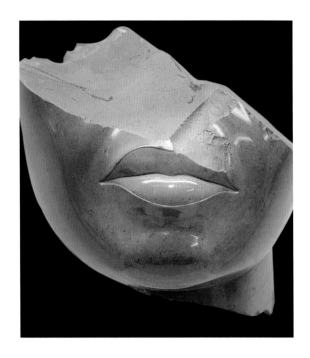

Alexander the Great was acclaimed as pharaoh of Egypt toward the end of 331 BCE. Welcomed by the Egyptians as a champion of their culture, the great conquerer set out on an eight-day pilgrimage to the oasis of Siwa and the oracle of Amun. Amun was the aspect of Ra as creator-god; to Alexander as to all other Greeks, he was Ammon-Zeus, the supreme Olympian deity.

On his arrival he made straight for the inner sanctum of the temple of Amun. There he asked three questions. There is no evidence of the nature of these questions (although a priest was said to have hidden himself in a false ceiling and so listened during Alexander's audience.) It is likely, however, that the new foreign pharaoh asked about his destiny; biographers have stated that the oracle proclaimed Alexander a god, and that he would indeed rule the world. This confirmation may have instilled Alexander to reject an offer from Darius, the king of Persia, to take the western domain of the empire rather than press on with the invasion. In the light of the oracle, perhaps, Alexander rejected the deal and his armies fought on, ultimately to conquer the entire country.

THE BOWL THAT SPEAKS

A LAMP IS LIT, using pure oil and a linen wick
A divining bowl is set by it, containing a measure of oil
A linen band is tied around the arm.

THIS TECHNIQUE is famous among mortals when they have dire need of answers.

An incantation is spoken aloud into the divining bowl, to summon the gods. Now the incantation is often a question, repeated solemnly several times, and it is spoken with the eyes closed. When the incantation is finished the inquirer opens his eyes, and the words of the gods will fill him. These divine words will be the answer to his question.

THE HOROSCOPE OF ANNU

Now I will reveal the horoscope of the gods, that which tells of my strange story as mortal and all the auspicious days by the three seasons of time. There are also auspicious days but with a warning. This is when one must proceed with caution. Those who are wise will take heed.

FIRST MONTH OF INUNDATION

The Days That Are Very Auspicious

August 1 The first day of the year. My great father of the sun, mighty Ra, ascends the horizon; there is the great festival of Opet as the waters of the Nile begin to rise.

August 2 The gods of Heliopolis go before Ra.

August 5 The gods are peaceful, steering the sky-boat of Ra on its course.

August 7 Mortals welcome the rising of the Nile and make offerings to the gods.

August 9 The day when every heart is at peace.

August 10 The festival of Hedj-Hotep, the goddess of weaving. Anyone born on this day will be respected in their twilight years.

August 18 The day on which Ra chose my son Horus over evil Set, and Horus was indeed honored with the white crown of Upper Egypt.

August 19 The festival of we gods of Heliopolis. Incense is burned by mortals in offering.

August 21 Mortals make offerings to the gods of Heliopolis; but they must avoid crossing paths with a bull, for this will bring ill-fortune.

August 24 Ra journeys through the firmament in peace. Anyone born on this day will be honored in old age.

August 27 The day of truce between Horus my

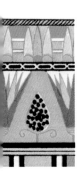

son and our enemy, Set. This day is declared a holiday.

August 28 The sight of Horus and Set pleases the gods.

August 30 The last day of the month. The festivals of Ra, Osiris, and Horus.

THE DAYS THAT ARE GENERALLY AUSPICIOUS, BUT WITH A WARNING

August 3 Yet anyone born on this day will meet their end by means of a crocodile.

August 4 But the gods (fortune) may go against you.

August 8 This day Ra goes forth. But do not venture out at night.

August 25 The day when the lioness Sekhmet journeyed East, and when the armies of Set did not triumph. Do not venture from your home at night.

August 29 Do not light a fire, burn incense, or go out at night.

SECOND MONTH OF INUNDATION

THE DAYS THAT ARE VERY AUSPICIOUS

August 31 The festival of the gods at Heliopolis.

September 1 Horus the Elder goes to his mother Nut. Mortals make offerings to all gods on this day.

September 2 The injured eye of my son, Horus, is healed by his love, Hathor.

September 5 Harmony is in the heavens and the gods celebrate. Anyone born on this day will die in a state of drunkenness.

September 7

September 8 The gods of Heliopolis enjoy festivities, and all enemies are vanquished. Anyone born on this day will be blessed with longevity.

September 9 The day of the procession of the cat-goddess Bast, my feline aunt.

September 10 The day of securing the front piece of the prow on the sacred boat of Ra.

September 12 The feast for the gods.

September 13 The day when my son Horus received the white crown; and all rejoice.

September 15 The feast-day of my beloved Osiris.

September 16 Mortals do offer the gods incense and beer on this day.

September 18 Nun of the watery chaos, my most ancient relative, goes forth to acknowledge the djed pillar, the sacred amulet of my husband Osiris.

September 27

September 28 Anyone born on this day will die respectable.

September 29 The last day of the month. The festivals of Ra, Osiris, and Horus.

Third Month of Inundation

THE DAYS THAT ARE VERY AUSPICIOUS
September 30 The day of the heavenly feast of my daughter-in-law, the goddess Hathor. A day for love.
October 2
October 5 The day of giving thanks to the gods of the two lands.
October 6
October 7 Isis' day of contentment; my son Horus is granted his just inheritance of the throne.
October 9 A day of rejoicing in heaven. The gods of Heliopolis smile; those in the fields are working.
October 10
October 11 A day of peace. The Eye of Horus is returned to the head of Ra.
October 15 The day when the gods of Heliopolis appear in Ashmuneim in Middle Egypt. It is a day of eternal happiness.
October 20 The day of the feast of my ancestor Shu, god of moisture.
October 21 The day of raising the statue of Maat, lady of truth, before Ra.
October 23 The day when I, Isis, went forth with joy in my heart and my sister Nephthys celebrates. We see Osiris, who has bequeathed his sovereignty to his rightful heir, our son Horus.
October 24
October 24 The day of conflict between Horus and Set. The djed pillar, amulet of Osiris, is placed in heaven; all Egypt is to be given to Horus, the desert to Set. Wise Thoth, god of morality, magic, and time, goes to make judgment before Ra.
October 26 The day of judging Set and Horus, and the end of their fighting.
October 27 The day when gods and mortals celebrate the decree written for Horus' kingship. There is great festivity.
October 28 The day when my son Horus is

given the white crown and Set is presented with the red crown. Both are satisfied.
October 29 The last day of the month. Day of the Houses of Horus, Ra, and Osiris.

Fourth Month of Inundation

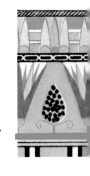

THE DAYS THAT ARE VERY AUSPICIOUS
October 30 Ra is joyful and Heliopolis celebrates. This is a day of fertility and procreation, for the primal instinct of Nun is in everyone.
October 31 The gods and the universe rejoice.
November 2 Mortals perform the rituals of Sobek, the crocodile water-god, in his temple and in their dwellings.
November 6
November 7 Thoth and the gods cause the defeat of Set. Avoid difficult situations today.
November 8 Anyone who is born on this day will die in old age with beer in his mouth.
November 9 The day of the feast of the reanimation of Osiris in Abydos. The dead rejoice.
November 11 The day of going forth of the White One, or Hathor. This is a day for rest from labor, for mingling with others and romance. Travel to foreign lands brings love.

ISIS IN THE TAROT

In the major arcana cards of the Tarot, Isis is represented as card II, The High Priestess. Some occultists, most prominently, Aleister Crowley, believed that Tarot cards were the magical Book of Thoth itself – the way to enlightenment and eternal life. The High Priestess card is the female mystic who stands before a veil that symbolizes the conscious and subconscious mind, or mundane and higher wisdom. Isis too, as supreme goddess of hidden knowledge, was associated with the veil. According to Plutarch, the statue of Isis at Sais bore the inscription, "I am all that has been, that is, and that will be, and no mortal has ever dared to lift my veil." Like Isis, the enigmatic High Priestess wears a blue cloak or gown, the color of spirituality.

November 12 The day on which I, Isis and my sister Nephthys fled from the weaving house where we were imprisoned by Set. We joyfully cast our tools into the Nile and the arms of Neith, the consort of watery Nun.
November 13 The feast-day of my aunts, the lioness Sekhmet and Bast the cat goddess.
November 28 The festivals of Ra, Osiris, and Horus. Mortals do make invocations and food offerings to the gods, who are happy.

THE DAYS THAT ARE MOSTLY AUSPICIOUS, BUT WITH A WARNING
November 3 The day when love-goddess Hathor goes forth before the gods of the ancient city of Kher-aba. She and the gods of Kher-aba and Heliopolis are honored with longevity and comfort. But beware of anyone who acts with base motive that may be sexual in nature.
November 20
November 21 The day when the enemies of Horus are poised to kill him. Stay indoors at night, for if you venture out and come upon a lion, you will die by it.
November 24
November 25 Anything you see today will be good. But do not go out at night.

FIRST MONTH OF EMERGENCE

THE DAYS THAT ARE VERY AUSPICIOUS
November 29 Double the offerings and present the gifts of Neb-kau, lord of the kas.
December 2 Anyone born on this day will die at an old age with his family around him.
December 6
December 7 The day when mortals make cakes soaked in beer to offer to Sekhmet, and then repeat their offerings to please the gods and spirits.
December 11 Day for praying for long life and worshipping Maat, the goddess of truth, in the temple.
December 13 The day of going forth of Nun where the gods are in primal darkness.
December 14 The day when Shu sends good dry air to the dead in their honor. A day when mortals make offerings and pay due respect to their ancestors.
December 16 The going forth of the gods to Abydos, the city of Osiris my beloved.
December 19 On this day my aunt Bast, goddess of cats, guards the two lands. Make offerings to the gods of Heliopolis.
December 20

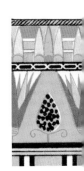

December 23 The day when Ra establishes the great cow in heaven. This is the banishment of my mother, Nut, to the sky and her sundering from my father Geb, whom Ra treads down to the earth. Take honey on this day, but do not drink milk.

SECOND MONTH OF EMERGENCE

THE DAYS THAT ARE VERY AUSPICIOUS
December 29 The feast-day celebrating the establishment of the world by the architect-god, Ptah. He lifts heaven with his two hands.
December 30 A day when the gods received Ra and everything in the universe was in its rightful place. The Two Lands celebrate.
January 1 Mortals perform acts of worship of their great ancestors on this day.
January 2
January 4 A day when mortals make offerings to the gods and spirits.
January 5 The day of the festival of the gods. Some mortals may make a pilgrimage to Letopolis, the sacred city of my son, Horus.
January 6 The day when the pharaoh as Horus decrees rations of food to those at the city of Kher-aba.
January 8 The feast day of Neith and of making Oracles. Writing materials are taken from the house of Neith to the house of her son, Sobek, at Crocodilopolis. There the people watch the movements of the sacred crocodiles, and transcribe them, and make oracles.
January 9
January 13 The day that I, Isis, received the true name of mighty Ra and the power of all creation. It is also the day that my son Horus defeated wily Set; so this is my day of joy.
January 14 The day of respect for the *wabet* of Osiris (his internal organs) which have been placed in the hands of Anubis for preservation.
January 19

December 21 Anyone born on this day will live a long and plentiful life.
December 22 Earth and heaven are in harmony.
December 25 The day of the great festival in Hefau, the land of the dead. The strength of Ra, the great sun, grows again as from this date the days become longer.
December 26 The day that wise god Thoth renews his allegiance to Ra in Ashmuneim, Middle Egypt. All mortals do celebrate and take a holiday on this day.
December 27 Bast and Sekhmet guide the two lands; the gods are happy.
December 28 The last day of the month. The festivals of Ra, Osiris, and Horus. Mortals offer incense to all the gods.

THE DAYS THAT ARE MOSTLY
AUSPICIOUS, BUT WITH A WARNING
November 30 A day of rest for mortals.
December 4 On this day mortals make double their food offerings to Wepwawet, he who opens the gates to the afterlife, and to Osiris. This day is good for furthering ambition but the seeker may find greed and opposition awaiting him.

January 20
January 22
January 23 The going forth of Min, the deity of fertility who is Amun and mighty Ra, to the city of Coptos. It is the day that Osiris impregnates me with our son, Horus.
January 24 The day of the feast of Sokar, god of the dead, in Rostau, the place of the pyramids before that of Osiris in Abydos.
January 25 Osiris is pleased and the spirits and the dead rejoice.

THE DAYS THAT ARE MOSTLY AUSPICIOUS, BUT WITH A WARNING
January 11 The day of the escape of Ra, of seeing the serpent, Apep, and killing him by the power of Set who guards the prow of the great barque of Ra. Do not go out at dawn on this day.
January 12 The gods pay tribute to Ra on his safe return. Ra pays tribute to Osiris and makes a ritual, offering to him the ankh and the *was*-scepter, that which is held by pharaohs.
January 18 The day of the reckoning of wealth. The cattle go to the meadows of the priests of the Temple of Karnak to be counted.

THIRD MONTH OF EMERGENCE

THE DAYS THAT ARE VERY AUSPICIOUS
January 28 The festival of the unification of the Two Lands. Horus is celebrated.
January 29
February 1 The day when Neith, goddess of war, goes forth from her city of Sais. In the night, her beauty is seen for four and one-half hours. Do not go out at this time or copulate, for you will be offended by others.
February 2 The Festival of Rebirth. The celebration of Osiris in Abydos and of the going forth of Anubis and his embalmers, who receive everyone. Mortals make penance on this day.

February 4 The creator-god Khnum makes ready for the emergence of the gods.
February 5 The day of judgment in Heliopolis.
February 8 The day that the Nile comes from Nun, the watery chaos from which all my family emerged. The river brings joy and food, so mortals offer food in thanks on this day.
February 9 The day that my uncle Thoth and his spirits go forth. Any ritual performed on this day will be auspicious.
February 14 The feast-day of my mother Nut, goddess of the sky. Mortals make a holiday on this day.
February 24 The day of the feast of my husband, beloved Osiris, in Abydos.
February 25
February 26 The last day of the month and a feast-day in Abydos. All is well, and there is the promise of immortality. The festivals of Ra, Osiris, and Horus.

THE DAY THAT IS MOSTLY AUSPICIOUS BUT WITH A WARNING
February 7 The Day of the Dead. The dead go about the necropolis to fend off the snake Apep. This brings danger to the fore but the dead do give spiritual succour to living mortals on this day.

FOURTH MONTH OF EMERGENCE

February 27 The day when the enemies of I, Isis, were defeated. There is a great feast in heaven.
February 29 The day that the priest of Geb goes to the throne of Abydos to see my nephew Anubis, god of funerary rites. There they talk of requirements, think for the number of tombs to be set.
March 2 The day the gods are satisfied when they see everything in its place in the heavens.
March 5 The day of going forth of Min, god of fertility. A day for love-making. The gods celebrate and mortals burn sweet myrrh incense on the fire.

THE EGYPTIAN ZODIAC

A curious postscript to the gory tale of Sekhmet (see pages 41–48) was found in the form of an intricately painted ceiling in the great Temple of Hathor at Dendera in central Egypt. It was discovered by French scholars brought by Napoleon in 1796 and now resides in the Louvre, Paris. The ceiling was painted in the time of the later Ptolemaic dynasty, possibly at the command of Queen Cleopatra herself. The ceiling is in the form of an astrological horoscope in which instead of the familiar twelve signs of the zodiac (as familiar to the people of the ancient Nile as they are to us) the gods of Egypt take their places in the celestial wheel.

The dating system used below has been adapted for modern use, along with a brief explanation of the astrological influence of each of the twelve gods. The dates begin at the annual flooding of the Nile, the beginning of the Egyptian year. This coincided with the return of the dog-star Sirius (the star of Isis) to the sky. It is therefore appropriate that Anubis, the dog- (or jackal-) headed deity commences the cycle.

Anubis	July 25–August 28	Determined, self-assured.
Thoth	August 19–September 27	Capable, wise, organized.
Horus	September 28–October 27	Confident, headstrong, obstinate.
Wadjet	October 28–November 26	Logical, dedicated, ambitious.
Sekhmet	November 27–December 26	Optimistic, eloquent, quarrelsome.
Horus of the Horizon (Sphinx)	December 27–January 25	Adaptable, disciplined, arrogant.
Shu	January 26–February 24	Cheerful, creative, indecisive.
Isis	February 25–March 26	Idealistic, intuitive, loyal.
Osiris	March 27–April 25	Witty, kindly, emotionally aloof.
Amun-Ra	April 26–May 25	Resolute, trustworthy, a leader
Hathor	May 26–June 24	Emotional, charming, romantic.
Bennu (Phoenix)	June 25–July 24	Resilient, busy, self-renewing.

March 6 The Eye of Horus is in its place and all its parts are accounted for. The gods of Heliopolis are delighted.

March 8 The complete Eye of Horus is introduced to the great gods. The power of Ra strengthens the gods

March 13 A happy day in the eastern horizon of heaven. The company of Heliopolis is instructed in the presence of the great ones in the two horizons.

March 14 The day of the going forth of Khepera the scarab. Every town rejoices.

March 17 A feast-day in Heliopolis. It is the day that Ra journeys in his barque across the firmament.

March 26

March 27 The day the gods are satisfied when they worship my husband Osiris. Mortals do burn incense on the fire and offer myrrh to their local gods.

March 28 The last day of the month. The festivals of Ra, Osiris, and Horus. Mortals make offerings to Ptah-Sokar-Osiris-Atum, lord of the Two Lands of Heliopolis, and to all the gods.

First Month of Summer

The Days That Are Very Auspicious

March 29 The feast-day of Horus, my son.

March 31

April 3 From the House of Ra the great gods come and rejoice. They and their followers receive the Eye of Horus.

April 4 The day when Horus defeats his enemy, Set. The dead look on. Every heart is happy.

April 5

April 6

April 14

April 15 The gods of Heliopolis and the dead rejoice.

April 16 All the gods rejoice on this day of counting by Thoth, who heard great Maat, goddess of truth.

April 19 Anyone born on this day will live a long life.

April 20

April 23

April 15

April 27 The last day of the month. House of Ra, House of Osiris, House of Horus.

Second Month of Summer

The Days That Are Very Auspicious

April 28

April 29 The gods listen. Those of the sun-boat of Ra are in festivity.

April 30 The beginning of the month of the followers of Ra. A feast-day on heaven and earth.

May 2

May 5 Mortals take a holiday for Ra and the gods of Heliopolis on this day.

May 6 An offering of incense of different sweet herbs is made by mortals to please Ra on this day.

May 7 Anyone born on this day will be noble.

May 9

May 10 The day of the feast of the Eye of Horus, or Wadjet-eye in Dep, the city of the cobra-goddess. There is singing and chanting, and mortals do make offerings of incense and sweet herbs.

May 11

May 13 Anyone born on this day will die a great and just lord.

May 20

May 21

May 22 The day that all are pacified by the Eye of Horus.

May 25 A day of purification and festivity of the gods. Mortals make offerings in Abydos, where Osiris my husband is worshipped.

May 26

May 27 The last day of the month. My ancestor Shu goes forth, so the air itself returns the Eye of Horus. Thoth appears. The festivals of Ra, Osiris, and Horus.

Third Month of Summer

The Days That Are Very Auspicious
May 28 A feast-day in southern heaven. Love-goddess Hathor, my daughter-in-law, celebrates with everyone.

May 29 A feast-day for all the gods.

May 31

June 5 A feast-day for all the gods. Peace is declared as the ravaging of my sister Sekhmet is quelled with blood-beer.

June 8 A holiday, the reception of Ra. Everyone celebrates.

June 11 My son Horus hears the words of the people in the presence of all the gods. In the dwellings of mortals, all good things occur.

June 17

June 20

June 22

June 25 The festival of Mut at the lake of the Temple of Karnak. Food is offered to the goddess and her followers at Thebes.

June 26 The last day of the month. The festivals of Ra, Osiris, and Horus.

The Day That is Mostly Auspicious, But With A Warning
June 21 The day that Set, that great enemy, is abroad at noon-time. Do not go out at this time.

Fourth Month of Summer

The Days That Are Very Auspicious
June 27 Mortals do make offerings to those in heaven on this day. And all gods partake in the feast of Osiris, my husband.

June 28 The day that Maat, she of Truth, and all the gods perform all proper rites. The universe is in harmony.

July 1 A day of temple festivities. The fertility god Min copulates at Akmim; so this is the day for conceiving a child.

July 4

July 5 Anyone born on this day will gain great respect.

July 6 The day that Set attacked great Ra at sunrise, and the great god repelled him. There is to be good fortune at sunrise.

July 8 The victory celebration throughout the land. The gods who dwell in their shrines are happy.

July 9 A holiday, celebrating the defending of my son, Horus, against my brother Set.

July 10

July 12 The day when mortals pour ritual water as an offering to their ancestors who have passed into the next world.

July 13

July 15 The day when the eye of Horus returns intact. Mortals do celebrate with feasts to their local gods.

July 17

July 18 The feast day of my nephew Anubis. We five children of Geb and Nut celebrate – I, Isis, Nephthys, Osiris, Horus the Elder and Set. It is a holiday because the gods are greatly purified on this day.

July 20 A holiday, when mortals make offerings to the gods.

July 21 The day that Ra shines supreme. One of the hottest days of the year.

July 24 The feast-day of the fertility-god, Min. A good time for love-making.

July 25 A holiday with festivities at the temple of the crocodile god Sokar in Memphis. The people there toast their health.

July 26 The last day of the year. Anything that occurs in Memphis or any other place today will be good, and will bode well for the coming year. Mortals sing and make many offerings to the gods.

THE DAY THAT IS MOSTLY AUSPICIOUS, BUT WITH A WARNING

July 22 It is the day that the gods sail to make the waters of the Nile rise. It is the approach of Sirius, the star of Isis. Do not venture out at noontime when the gods sail through the heavens.

THE FIVE ADDITIONAL DAYS OF THE YEAR

Now when any mortal on earth is versed in the names of the five additional days of the year, those that wise Thoth stole from the moon-god

Khonsu, will have favor for all their lives. They shall eat and drink in plenty; and even my sultry aunt Bast, queen of seductresses, will not corrupt him. No enemy will harm him, and Maat shall be with him and he will come before no court in the land. He will prosper indeed, and mighty Ra, my great father, will hear his words.

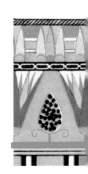

FIRST DAY
July 27 The birth of beloved Osiris, my husband. Say these words: O Osiris, bull in his cavern, whose name is hidden...Hail to thee; I am thy son, O father Osiris. The name of this day is The Pure One...

SECOND DAY
July 28 The birth of Horus, my brother. Say these words: O Horus of Letopolis... The name of this day is Mighty is the Heart.

THIRD DAY
July 29 The birth of my red-haired brother, wily Set. Say these words: O Set, son of Nut, great of strength... protection is at the hands of thy holiness. I am thy son. The name of this day is He Who Makes Terror.

FOURTH DAY
July 30 The day of my birth, great Isis. Say these words to me: O this Isis, daughter of Nut, the eldest, mistress of magic, provider of the book, mistress who appeases the two lords, her face is glorious. I am the brother and sister. The name of this day is Powerful of Heart.

FIFTH DAY
July 31 The birth of Nephthys, my dark sister. Say these words: O Nephthys, daughter of Nut, sister of Set, she whose father sees a healthy daughter...I am the divine power in the womb of my mother Nut. The name of this day is The Child Who is in his Nest.

After these five days, this spell is chanted to call upon our protection.

THE CAIRO CALENDAR

In 1943, the three volumes of papyri were purchased by the Cairo Museum from an antiquities dealer. Two of the volumes were badly damaged and undecipherable, but one volume presented an almost complete summary of Egyptian festivals with daily predictions for every day of the year. This papyrus has since become known as the Cairo Calendar, which has been reinterpreted here (see pages 131–141). In modern times the New Year can be said to begin on August 1, because this coincides with the rise of the star Sirius and the annual Inundation of the Nile, but in ancient times the rise of Sirius and hence, New Year's day, occurred on June 21. Some interpretations of the calendar therefore begin on this day.

The calendar celebrates the lives of its principle gods and goddesses, attributing mythological significance to certain dates and at times adding advice. However, some readings may record historical events, such as that for July 6. This was the day when Set attacked Ra, and was defeated; however, this coincides with the invasion of the so-called "Sea-People" who were probably migrant Minoans from the island of Crete, whom Ramesses III (1184–1153 BCE) of the twentieth dynasty repelled from the Syria and the Egyptian Delta. His victories were recorded on the walls of Ramesses III's mortuary temple at Medinet Habu near to the Valley of the Kings.

Instructions and predictions for the day are also given. This varies from making the right offerings to the gods or one's dead ancestors, such as burning incense or making a water libation. Here, the auspicious and mostly auspicious days are included. Dates that have been omitted are those that were unreadable on the original papyrus, or they are days that were considered adverse. There is a multitude of warnings for each of the adverse days, from dying of blindness or in foreign lands to suffering a skin rash. Death by crocodile was a popular warning, but surely the most remarkable was death by copulation – perhaps the most pleasant way to get to the afterlife.

THE AMULET OF THE KNOT OF ISIS

THIS IS MY AMULET, the Knot of Isis, or Tyet. It is the key to traveling about the Land of the Dead, for it gives the bearer the magical power to go wheresoever they wish. But it is imbued with my feminine power, so is celebrated as a talisman of strong protection and fertility, my own qualities.

Here is the incantation that must be spoken over my knot, to dedicate it to me. It must be of red jasper or carnelian, or another red stone, for this represents my life-blood, and will keep safe any mortal who wears it around their neck or at the waist.

THE BLOOD of Isis
The spells of Isis
The magical powers of Isis

Shall make this great one strong
and shall be an amulet of protection
against any that would do him wrong.

At the first hour of night is eerie light; and jackal-headed Wepwawet, so like my nephew Anubis but pale and ashen, stands guard as the opener of the way to the Land of the Dead. And from this mouth of the underworld the barque of cold Ra inches onward.

The second hour approaches, and our barque eases along a narrow passage of the river by the tallest gate. It is constricted like a tight throat, guarded by a venomous serpent with his two companions, and all three spit flames and noxious evil poisons. And so the goddess of the second hour speaks aloud the name of the head serpent; and the roaring of the serpents ceases and they become as quiet as wax figures before the might of her spell. The gate gapes wide to allow our divine cargo to enter the country of Ur-nes or "Starry Heaven"; here dwells peace and happy god Bes, with Nepra and Tepu-yn, the spirits of fertility and wheat. In their name do I dedicate this next amulet, the Scepter of Papyrus, for it speaks of natural creation. It is placed on the neck of the deceased, as this is where we are at this point in our journey. But mortals do make it in miniature, from a kind of emerald, or blue or green porcelain, for it brings vigor. The following is inscribed on the amulet or chanted over it, to grant fertility and new life.

The Amulet of the Scepter of Papyrus, for Youth

O YOU WHO HAVE come forth today
   from the god's house
She whose voice is strong and mighty goes
   round about from the door of the Two
   Houses
she has assumed the very power of her
   father,
who is ennobled as Bull of the Nursing
   Goddess
and she accepts those of her followers who
   do great deeds for her.

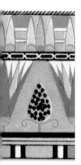

In truth my favored hours of night (if I was forced to choose any) are the third hour, where sits my husband Osiris in adoration and in judgment of the hearts of all men. And also the seventh, for this is when I practice magic supreme in the Secret Cavern, the lair of Apep himself. For he is the most dread, dark, hateful and perilous serpent who dwells in the most noisome region of the dark land.

Now the third hour of night is the realm of the heart; for the barque has already journeyed from the cavernous mouth of the afterlife through the narrow throat of the second gate, and now we reach the moral domain of this fearsome land. For it is the heart, not the brain, that is the conscience of mankind. Here men have the greatest trepidation, for mighty enthroned Osiris decrees their fate by weighing the heart against the feather of truth of Maat, she of Justice.

Ordinary mortals and priests who discourse with the gods wear the amulet of the heart, for it evokes the divine protection of Osiris and Ra for all those who dwell in the afterlife and all those who live under the sun. This prayer is to be recited over a heart of carnelian, although hearts can be made of many stones. Some decorate their amulets with the Bennu-bird [heron or phoenix], for it is associated with Osiris and Ra; and the sacred scarab, that is Kephera or Ra in his aspect at dawn.

THE NAMES OF THE TWELVE HOURS OF NIGHT

The first hour: The Watercourse of Ra. The home of six fire-breathing serpents, who light the way for the boat.

The second hour: The Starry Heaven, where three snakes breathe fire and poison.

The third hour: The Watercourse of the Only God; the kingdom of Osiris. The hour of judgment, when the hearts of mortals are deemed to be good or wicked.

The fourth hour: The Living One of Forms; kingdom of Osiris. domain of angry snakes.

The fifth hour: Hidden: ruled by Sokar, a mummified falcon. The scarab Kephera alights on the chest of Ra.

The sixth hour: Abyss of the Waters; ruled by Osiris, who is worshipped here as a god of fertility. Kephera flies to rest in the coils of a five-headed serpent.

The seventh hour: The Secret Cavern, home of the serpent Apep whom Isis defeats with the aid of Selket, the scorpion-goddess, and Mehen, the great cobra.

The eighth hour: The Sarcophagus of the Gods, the home of the souls of dead gods.

The ninth hour: The Procession of Images. The home of the twelve star-gods, who help paddle the boat to the tenth gate.

The tenth hour: Abyss of Waters, Lofty of Banks. Kephera unites with Ra, and Ra is renewed with life.

The eleventh hour: The Mouth of the Cavern. Horus the vengeful presides over the suffering of the wicked in the pits of fire.

The twelfth hour: Darkness Has Fallen and Births Shine Forth. Ra becomes Kephera. His old body is thrown from the boat and the new Ra stands strong, illuminating the universe at dawn.

THE AMULET OF THE HEART, FOR PROTECTION EVERMORE

I AM THE BENNU, the soul of Ra
and the guide of the gods who are in the underworld.
Their divine souls came forth upon earth
to do the will of their doubles,
Let therefore the soul of Osiris come forth
to do the will of his double [other self].

THE AMULET OF THE SCARAB, FOR TAKING HEART

WHEN A HEART is broken, the spirit must rise anew and cast aside the old heart that is empty like a drum. Then a mortal must take on the universe and all its troubles once again. The ritual I here present is for those who must take heart; it will give strength with the promise of re-birth and hope.

The scarab-beetle amulets of some mortals show an engraving of the human heart, just as a heart amulet may carry the image of the scarab-beetle, for the two are as one. But there is procedure for the wearing of a scarab, which must be followed.

A scarab-beetle, of precious emerald or green jade is taken and a gold wire is passed through it. The name of I, holy Isis, is carved upon it:

THE DJED AMULET, FOR STRENGTH

THE DJED is the amulet of Osiris. It is held in awe throughout the Two Lands, for it speaks of the reconstitution of the body of Osiris and thus tells of the greatest magic of mine. This cruciform pillar of three or four cross-bars is sacred not only to my husband but also to Sokar and to Ptah. But in the main it is held to represent both the backbone of my beloved husband and the very pillar in which his body was concealed in Byblos. The potent virtue of this talisman is that is bestows stability and endurance. For mortals, it brings strength at times of opposition. Here is a prayer to be incanted over the precious Djed.

RISE UP THOU, O Osiris!
You have your backbone, O still-heart!
You have the fastenings of your neck and back, O still-heart!
Place yourself upon your base
I put water beneath you
and I bring unto you a Djed of gold
that you may rejoice therein.

THE DJED, PILLAR OF OSIRIS

The Djed is shaped as a column with ridges to represent the spine of Osiris. Its alternative name as the Pillar of Osiris relates to the Isis and Osiris myth when the body of Osiris is imprisoned in a tree trunk that is used as a pillar in the mansion of a king – with Osiris intact within (pages 60–62).

The Djed (sometimes called a Tet) is a symbol of divine power, typically found as a funerary amulet on mummies. In the British Museum, an elaborate Djed can be seen painted on the back of the coffin of Itineb, a noble of the twenty-sixth dynasty or later. The Djed is shown with human eyes and torso, painted in green, holding the crook and flail of Osiris. Above it is the standard Djed column, crowned with a sun-disk and two protective cobras.

From the two-chambered realm of the heart we journey on toward the fourth, a deep and dry ravine with sand and dire howling wind. And at the command of the fourth goddess, the very barque of Ra is transformed into a majestic serpent that carries us upon his back. Here our snake is a fierce protector, ever-vigilant for the rasp of armour-like scales and hateful slither of vile Apep who at any moment may come forth from his lair to stalk us.

Yet in safety the fifth hour is reached, the domain of boiling lakes where the evil suffer the torments of their just punishment. I confess I am surely grateful when the sixth hour is upon us and our snake-boat is transformed back into the bejeweled barque of glory, and we are once again on the meandering river of night. For here, my beloved Osiris stands tall, and is worshipped for the fertility he bestows. This domain of my husband brings me comfort and courage before I must undergo battle with Apep in the next realm of black horror.

NOW A MENTION ASIDE ABOUT VILE APEP.

He truly has little to occupy him other than supply nightly torment for one hour. Yet all his venomous anger is contained within it, for when his fury rises and his slithering form unfurls, he is a fearsome hungry beast, a tyrant of great malice. My task to do battle with this monster is perhaps my most perilous assignment; my most onerous burden, but then as I have told earlier, I possess the secret name of Ra himself, so it is only fitting that I take this, the greatest of risks.

As the barque of Ra nudges the banks of the seventh realm, that of the very depths and entrails of existence, I espy the festering sand bank that is Apep's lair. It measures four hundred and fifty cubits in gory length and is fetid with the monster's filth.

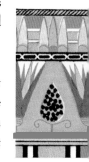

I am dressed in finery and bear the crown of the Two Lands upon my defiant brow, with steely Nekhbet, the vulture-goddess and Wadjet, she of the cobra, encircled about my head. These two are the guardians of me and my son, Horus, and of Upper and Lower Egypt. With Nekbhet's wings wrapped around me, I am ever protected. I clutch the Ankh, the symbol that is All Life, and the Eye of Horus, that I hold while I recite my first spell.

AND I NOW SPEAK THE TERRIBLE WORDS OF POWER.

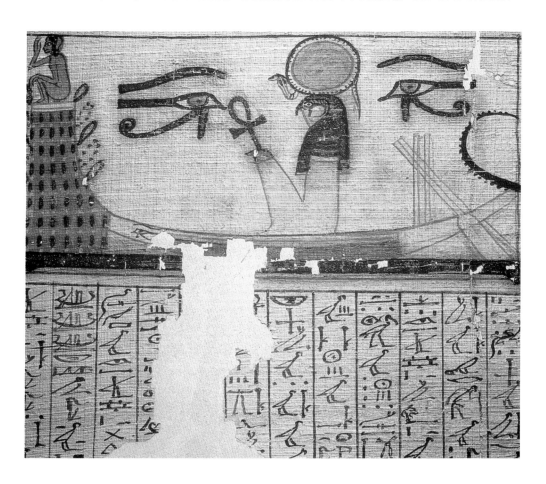

The Spell for Passing Safely by the Perilous Coils of Apep

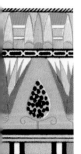

O YOU WAXEN ONE who takes by robbery and who
lives on the dead
I will not be inert for you, I will not be weak for you,
your poison shall not enter into my limbs,
for my limbs are the limbs of Atum [Ra]…
I am Atum at the head of the Abyss
my protection is from the gods, the lords of eternity
I am He whose name is secret…
I have gone forth with Atum, I am one who is not examined
I am hale, I am hale!

WITH THIS SPELL I also call upon my amulet of the
Serpent's Head, for now Apep arises in fearsome form and his
ragged jaws stretch like an abyss, rearing with sharpened fangs
dripping mordant venom and possessed of an appetite to fill his
cavernous, scaly belly with the barque of Ra and all it carries.
And I curse him, and speak the secret spells again and again.
These incantations are great secrets so I will not tell of them
here, but mortals do chant this little cantrip with their serpent-
headed talismans, in memory of me.

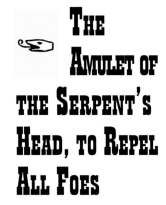

The Amulet of the Serpent's Head, to Repel All Foes

O SERPENT! I am the
  flame that shines
upon the opener of
  hundreds of thousands
  of years
and the standard of young
  plants and flowers.
Depart from me, for I am
  the divine lynx.

The barque now trembles at the tip of the tongue of ravenous Apep, poised to strike with his
poisonous fangs. His eyes are two green lamps of envious famishment as he rears again before
me. I am so small before this vast monster but in my heart I know my knowledge and power to
be the greater.

I raise my hands and evoke my divine protectors: Mehen the cobra, who opens his mighty
hood to shield Ra in his barque; and the scorpion-goddess Selket, and ram-headed Herishef
(one of the strongest and most heroic of the gods), who fall on Apep with their spears and
knives. As they fight the deadly spirit of the serpent, I cast spells of binding. There these two
deities remain, bearing down upon Apep, holding him fast so the barque can skirt around his
coils and onward through the other realms of the night.

Yet the serpent will only succumb to my magic enough to immobilize him. He is immortal and can never die, which is why I must endure this ordeal night after night forever more.

So onward goes the boat of Ra through the remaining five Kingdoms of the Night, through regions where dwell past pharaohs and the mighty of Egypt, onward through the houses of the star gods and pits where suffer the damned. Until at last the scarab Khepera reunites with the very body of the recumbent sun god, and at the very Mouth of the Cavern Ra is restored to life everlasting, for Darkness is Conquered and the world is renewed. Hail to Ra, the bright one, he who is Khepera in the morning restoring life to the earth and gladness to the hearts of men.

THE ANKH

The well-known talisman of the ankh was regarded by the Romans as the Cruz Ansata or Cross of Isis; early Christians saw it as a forerunner of the Crucifix. However, the ankh represents a humble sandal strap seen from above. The loop would have passed around the ankle while the long vertical line represents the leather thong that rested between the toes.

The primary meaning of the symbol is life. For this reason Horus, Ra, and Isis herself are often to be seen holding the ankh to the lips of the deceased pharaoh to grant him a new existence free of worldly care. It will be remembered that Isis had tricked the sun-god Ra into revealing his secret name to her so that she shared in the power of creation. Perhaps this is the reason that the ankh is more closely associated with Isis than with any other deity.

In later times, the symbol was taken up by believers in reincarnation. They saw the horizontal line as representing the earthly plane of existence. The vertical line was said to symbolize the ascent of the soul through animal to human forms, while the loop lifted the spirit into heavenly realms before returning it once more to be born again on earth.

The Amulets of Isis

For All Else

Here are more of my amulets; but let it be known that there are more than seventy. They are designed in miniature of the original to aid every aspect of mortal and immortal life. The more precious the mineral from which they are made, the better; for the color of an amulet does make its power greater. If this is not possible, take any green stone that is pleasing to the eye, as the first amulets were fashioned from such material. And surely they were magically potent and still work to this day.

The Amulet of the Pillow.
For help and support, as this is the symbol of the headrest of the mummy that uplifts it. Of hematite.

The Amulet of the Golden Collar.
For independence. Of gold.

The Amulet of the Ladder.
To get to heaven and follow your dreams. Of wood.

The Nefer Amulet.
For happiness and beauty. Of red stone, such as carnelian or red porcelain. It is often made as a necklace-pendant.

The Menat Amulet.
For health, fertility, and the unifying of men and women.
Of bronze, stone, porcelain and more. To be worn about the neck or held in the hand. A favorite of gods, kings, and priests.

The Amulet of the Shen.
For eternity. But it also has the meaning of moving forward in life. Of lapis lazuli or carnelian.

The Amulets of Anubis and Bast, For Finding a Lost Cat or Dog

Now my nephew Anubis, he of funereal rites, is soft hearted and will supply his help to find both cats and dogs who have strayed from their master. Some mortals, who wish to find a lost cat, call upon my dear aunt Bast, she who is supreme goddess of the feline race. But Anubis will also suffice if a mortal has such misfortune as to lose both, for his amulet will return these creatures, all safe and sound.

Make a tiny figure of Anubis or of Bast, from clay and place it around the neck of the animal. Wish that Anubis or Bast give their unending protection.

OR

Write the words Anubis or Bast on papyrus, or draw a simple image of these deities using vegetable ink. Fold it very small and set it beneath the creature's collar, so as not to cause discomfort. This papyrus is your amulet.

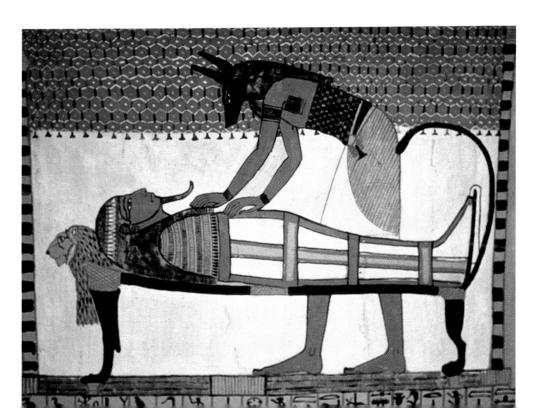

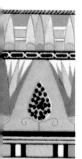

There are two more symbols I impart to you, for they tell part of my story, and by them will you recognize me and my sister Nephthys, wherever we may be. You will know us:

By The Bowl.

The bowl is the symbol of my sister Nephthys. She is called Lady of the Mansion, and is seen in her sculpted form holding aloft an empty bowl. At her temple in Kom Mer in Upper Egypt, she is known as Anuket, as I, Isis, am sometimes known as Auset.

By The Empty Throne.

The empty throne is mine, for when I sought out Osiris the people depicted me carrying on my crown the empty throne of my husband. And so it became a symbol of my quest. It also showed the people how the descent of rulers comes through a woman, not a man; so in a sense I carried the throne as I carried the line of rulers and gods. For I am Isis, she of the many names, mother of kings, wife of the greatest of gods, speaker of words of power and possessor of the greatest secret of all, the very name that caused the universe to come into being.

These are the very words of Isis.

Index

Published by Cico Books Ltd
32 Great Sutton Street
London EC1V 0NB

© Cico Books Ltd 2003
© Text copyright Jonathan Dee 2003

10 9 8 7 6 5 4 3 2 1

A CIP catalogue record for this book is available from the British Library.

ISBN 1 903116 60 0
Designed by David Fordham
Printed in Singapore